HAWKEYES 2002

A SEASON TO REMEMBER

The Daily Iowan

SP
SPORTS
PUBLISHING
L.L.C.

www.SportsPublishingLLC.com

Officially Licensed by the University of Iowa

SPORTS PUBLISHING L.L.C

Publisher
PETER L. BANNON

Senior Managing Editors
SUSAN M. MOYER and JOSEPH J. BANNON, JR.

Coordinating Editor
NOAH A. AMSTADTER

Art Director
K. JEFFREY HIGGERSON

Interior Design
TRACY GAUDREAU

Cover Design
KENNETH J. OBRIEN

Book Layout
TRACY GAUDREAU and JENNIFER L. POLSON

Imaging
**CHRISTINE MOHRBACHER, KERRI BAKER
and ERIN LINDEN-LEVY**

Copy Editor
CYNTHIA L. MCNEW

THE DAILY IOWAN

Publisher
WILLIAM CASEY

Editor
RYAN J. FOLEY

Sports Editor
ROSEANNA SMITH

Football Writer
TODD BROMMELKAMP

Photo Editor
ZACH BOYDEN-HOLMES

© The Daily Iowan

All Rights Reserved. No part of this book may be reproduced in any form or by any electronic or mechanical means including information storage and retrieval systems—except in the case of brief quotations embodied in critical articles or reviews—without permission in writing from its publisher, Sports Publishing L.L.C.

All stories and photographs are from the files of *The Daily Iowan*.

Front Cover Photo: Andy King, AP/Wide World Photos
Back Cover Photo: Curtis Lehmkuhl/The Daily Iowan

ISBN 1-58261-666-3

Lucas Underwood/The Daily Iowan

Lucas Underwood/The Daily Iowan

EDITOR'S NOTE

Dear Hawkeyes:

When we published a point-counterpoint on Sept. 24 debating the question "Can Iowa's Football Team Win the Big Ten Title?" I almost chuckled. Although the Hawks had smoked Utah State two days earlier, I did not think they could do the same on the road at Penn State or Michigan.

But not only did the team win the Big Ten title, they did so without a loss. For the first time in 80 years, the team sailed through the Big Ten undefeated. What a season!

The story of the season is more than just on-the-field success. The team overcame some off-the-field legal problems. Coach Kirk Ferentz quieted many who questioned both his ability as coach and the size of his salary package. Brad Banks went from being a little-known backup to a Heisman Trophy contender.

It was a great year to cover the Hawks. Two of my goals as editor were to improve both photography and the use of our Web site, and the team's success made both of those easy to achieve. We set aside a page in our paper every Monday for photos and updated the site with stories and slide shows of photos after every game.

But I must give props where props are due. Reporter Todd Brommelkamp tirelessly covered the team, detailing every new development while giving insight and sharing the player's stories. The photography staff as a whole did an excellent job capturing the moments that truly defined the Hawkeyes' success.

We are proud to display that success in the pages that follow.

Ryan J. Foley

Ryan J. Foley
Editor, *The Daily Iowan*

Lucas Underwood/The Daily Iowan

“
*IT FEELS GOOD TO BE
WHERE WE'RE AT RIGHT
NOW. OUR HARD WORK
DEFINITELY PAID
OFF FOR US.*
”

—Hawkeyes Quarterback
Brad Banks

LEFT:

Brad Banks high-steps into the end zone against
Northwestern on Nov. 9 for the first of his two
rushing scores on the day. The senior accounted
for three touchdowns on 10-10 passing. Lucas
Underwood/The Daily Iowan

STARTING OVER

After distraction-filled off season, Ferentz's focus shifts to the field

BY TODD BROMMELKAMP
DAILY IOWAN ASSISTANT SPORTS EDITOR

One of Kirk Ferentz's off-season goals for the Iowa football team was to avoid any public distractions. Iowa's head football coach can only hope the team tackles his other objectives for the 2002 season in a more proper manner than it did when it came to staying out of the headlines.

"Obviously, we've come up very short in that area," Ferentz told the media earlier this month prior to the break of camp.

"We've opened the door to [attention] through our own actions."

The team battled a variety of negative off-field incidents that ranged from possession of alcohol under the legal age to possession of marijuana to OWI to disorderly conduct. The summer's debauchery culminated with the dismissal of Benny Sapp for an early August incident in which the former starting cornerback was charged with three misdemeanors, including public intoxication.

"It's a new start," Ferentz said after Sapp's expulsion. "What I'm concerned about is how our players respond to this."

So far, so good for the 105 Hawkeye members preparing to open the season Saturday against Akron. The only headlines the team is grabbing these days are about its progress on the field, and that's just the way it should be for a team coming off its first winning season and bowl appearance since 1997.

"For the first time, we really feel like the field leveled out for us [last season]," Ferentz said. "We feel we have a lot of good, young players coming up."

The development of many of those players will be vital to a Hawkeye team that suffered key losses at all three skill positions. Ferentz will look for quarterback Brad Banks, running back Aaron Greving, and a host of talented yet young receivers to replace departed starters Kyle McCann, Ladell Betts, and Kahlil Hill.

Ferentz says Banks, who passed for 582 yards behind McCann a year ago, has a strong hold on the No. 1 spot ahead of JC transfer Nathan Chandler. Greving stole the spotlight in Iowa's Alamo Bowl victory, rushing for 115 yards in place of an injured Betts. C. J. Jones, Mo Brown, and Ramon Ochoa are the only upperclassmen with experience at receiver, and they will be joined by Warren Holloway and Ed Hinkel in the hunt to become Iowa's featured wideout.

On the other side of the ball, the Hawkeyes must fill the void left by three experienced and talented defensive linemen in Aaron Kampman, Jerry Montgomery, and Alamo Bowl Defensive MVP Derrick Pickens. All played key parts in a defensive line that held four Big Ten foes to under 100 yards rushing. Howard Hodges, Jared Clauss, and Jonathan Babineaux are the front-runners on the current depth chart. Redshirt freshman Antwan Allen will fill the void in Iowa's secondary created by Sapp's departure.

ABOVE: *Then-junior quarterback Brad Banks drops back for a pass during Iowa's spring game at Kinnick Stadium on April 20, 2002.* Scott Morgan/The Daily Iowan

While the players who exited made a big impression on the field during Iowa's 7-5 campaign a year ago, they had an even bigger effect off the field.

"We had a great group of seniors last year, and they did a great job of giving us leadership," he said. "That's probably our No. 1 challenge this year to replace."

Veterans such as defensive tackle Colin Cole say they are ready to meet the call for guidance.

"I've always had a great group of guys to look up to," Cole said. "Now, Coach tells us it's our time, our turn to lead."

One area where the Hawkeyes have few questions is the offensive line—the team lost just one senior, Alonzo Cunningham, to graduation. Guard Andy Lightfoot, who started five games a year ago, joins line veterans Robert Gallery, Eric Steinbach, Bruce Nelson, and David Porter to provide Iowa with a line that will rival any in the school's recent history, Ferentz said.

"On the field, the O-line sets the tempo for everything," said Porter, who was granted an extra year of eligibility for medical reasons. "We spend a lot of time away from the field together, and on the field, it makes the chemistry that much stronger."

Not surprisingly, the least-talked-about area on the team may be the squad's biggest concern: its special teams performance. While kicker Nate Kaeding proved to have one of the most reliable feet in the Big Ten, first-year punter David Bradley struggled, averaging just over 36 yards per punt. The team also lost its top punt and kick returner in Hill, who won the Mosi Tatupu award as special teams Player of the Year in 2001. But the biggest question mark will still be punting, something Ferentz expected to deal with a year ago and will again show some patience with this year.

"You lose a guy like [former Iowa punter Jason Baker], and you just don't replace him with a freshman," Ferentz said. "Our special teams are going to be better from what I saw this spring."

Between the key losses and question marks, it's easy to see why the so-called experts have picked the Hawkeyes to finish anywhere from sixth to 10th in the league, and that sits just fine with Ferentz. He feels that with the right adjustments, the Hawkeyes can find themselves competing for a spot in the league's upper echelon when it matters most.

"I think the goal for everyone is to be there in November, so yeah, I think it's realistic given that we make improvement in the areas where we need it."

Iowa's season opener is slated for an 11 a.m. start at Kinnick Stadium on Saturday.

LEFT:

Fred Russell looks for open running room during Iowa's April spring game. Scott Morgan/The Daily Iowan

Lucas Underwood/The Daily Iowan

SATURDAY, AUGUST 31, 2002
AKRON ZIPS 21 AT IOWA HAWKEYES 57

HAWKS 'ZIP' PAST AKRON IN OPENER

Backups Russell, Lewis run past Zips in 57-21 win

BY TODD BROMMELKAMP
DAILY IOWAN ASSISTANT SPORTS EDITOR

It turns out the Iowa Hawkeyes didn't need Aaron Greving after all. As a matter of fact, there wasn't much the Hawkeyes needed on Saturday, Aug. 31.

Iowa racked up nearly 600 yards of total offense in a 57-21 rout of the Akron Zips at Kinnick Stadium.

Backup running backs Fred Russell and Jermelle Lewis, playing in place of the injured Greving, each rushed for more than 100 yards in the first significant amount of playing time for either player. Russell ran for 170 yards and two touchdowns, and Lewis cruised for 123 yards and a pair of scores.

BELOW: *Derek Pagel takes down Akron's Nick Fortener during Iowa's win over Akron. Pagel had five solo tackles on the day.*
Ben Plank/The Daily Iowan

ABOVE: *Quarterback Brad Banks tosses a shovel pass to avoid being sacked. Banks completed five of his eight pass attempts for 125 yards and two touchdowns.* Zach Boyden-Holmes/The Daily Iowan

"Fred is someone we've been really excited about, and he performed really well today," Iowa coach Kirk Ferentz said. "We've been talking about [Jermelle] over the last two years, and today, it was good for him to get out and actually perform on the field."

Russell scored his first touchdown of the day on Iowa's first drive of the game, slashing through the Akron defense for a 44-yard score. It was the first seven of a record-breaking 37 points scored by the Hawkeyes in the first quarter alone, besting the previous school mark for scoring in a single quarter of 35 points set against Illinois in 1985. Russell sandwiched another touchdown run of 35 yards around a 72-yard fumble return for a score by linebacker Kevin Worthy and a safety.

A pair of touchdown tosses to Mo Brown on Iowa's final two possessions of the first quarter put the game well out of hand for the Zips.

ABOVE: *Fred Russell eludes an outstretched Zips defender en route to the end zone. Russell totaled 172 yards to go along with two touchdowns.* Zach Boyden-Holmes/The Daily Iowan

"I was surprised that they scored as much as they did, but I wasn't surprised that they came out ripping and roaring," said Akron coach Lee Owens.

Akron reached the board in the second quarter when Charlie Frye connected with Matt Cherry for a seven-yard scoring strike, but Lewis answered with back-to-back touchdown runs of one and two yards respectively.

"You could have gotten a truck through some of those holes they had," Iowa quarterback Brad Banks said.

Much of the credit goes to the members of the Iowa offensive line, who created those openings and did not allow a quarterback sack. Despite their request for no interviews after the game, their performance as a whole did not go unrecognized by teammates.

"There were times when the first guy I saw was in the secondary," Lewis said.

	1st	2nd	3rd	4th	Final
AKRON	0	14	7	0	21
IOWA	37	14	3	3	57

SCORING SUMMARY

QTR	TEAM	PLAY		TIME
1st	**HAWKEYES**	TD	Russell 44-yd. run (Kaeding kick)	13:01
1st	**HAWKEYES**	TD	Worthy 72-yd. fumble recovery (Kaeding kick)	10:26
1st	**HAWKEYES**	ST	Team Safety	9:29
1st	**HAWKEYES**	TD	Russell 35-yd. run (Kaeding kick)	8:10
1st	**HAWKEYES**	TD	Brown 56-yd. pass from Banks (Kaeding kick)	5:02
1st	**HAWKEYES**	TD	Brown 36-yd. pass from Banks (Kaeding kick)	0:10
2nd	**ZIPS**	TD	Cherry 7-yd. pass from Frye (Sullivan kick)	11:54
2nd	**HAWKEYES**	TD	Lewis 1-yd. run (Kaeding kick)	9:39
2nd	**HAWKEYES**	TD	Lewis 2-yd. run (Kaeding kick)	3:06
2nd	**ZIPS**	TD	Goodwin 31-yd. pass from Frye (Sullivan kick)	0:00
3rd	**HAWKEYES**	FG	Kaeding 23-yd.	12:30
3rd	**ZIPS**	TD	Payne 1-yd. run (Sullivan kick)	7:35
4th	**HAWKEYES**	FG	Kaeding 20-yd.	13:36

OFFENSE

ZIPS

PASSING	ATT	COMP	YDS	INT	TD
Frye	29	21	230	0	2
Sparks	9	7	66	1	0

RECEIVING	CATCHES	YDS	TD
Cherry	8	68	1
Payne	4	52	0
Basch	4	48	0
Irvin	4	31	0
Sparks	3	31	0
Goodwin	1	31	1
Fortener	1	16	0
Szakos	1	9	0
Ringer	1	6	0
Washington	1	4	0

RUSHING	RUSHES	YDS	TD
Payne	14	32	1
Ringer	4	14	0
Barbee	3	13	0
Basch	3	12	0
Washington	2	11	0
Frye	5	4	0
Sparks	3	2	0
McCray	1	-1	0

HAWKEYES

PASSING	ATT	COMP	YDS	INT	TD
Chandler	12	7	92	0	0
Banks	8	5	125	0	2

RECEIVING	CATCHES	YDS	TD
Brown	3	102	2
Solomon	2	34	0
Ochoa	2	26	0
Jones	1	20	0
Lewis	1	11	0
Russell	1	11	0
Clark	1	8	0
Hinkel	1	5	0

RUSHING	RUSHES	YDS	TD
Russell	14	170	2
Lewis	19	123	2
Jones	1	25	0
Schnoor	4	24	0
Cervantes	2	12	0
Mangan	1	8	0
Sherlock	1	5	0
Chandler	1	5	0
Banks	2	4	0

In his debut as Iowa's starting quarterback, Banks completed five of eight attempts for 125 yards, including the pair of scores to Brown. But the success of Iowa's ground attack meant that the Hawks didn't need many passes. Backup Nathan Chandler was equally irrelevant, completing seven of twelve tosses for 92 yards.

Both quarterbacks had plenty of options on offense; seven different Hawkeyes rushed for positive yardage, and eight different Hawks caught passes. Brown was the team's leading receiver with 102 yards and two scores on just three catches.

With Iowa leading, 51-14, at the half and the game well in hand, the second half was a lackluster affair in which both teams emptied their benches in order to get younger players onto the field.

With Akron starting quarterback Charlie Frye sidelined because of dehydration, the Zips managed just one score in the second half, a one-yard run by Brandon Payne in the third quarter, while Iowa tacked on a pair of field goals by Nate Kaeding.

BELOW: Hawkeyes receiver Maurice Brown gets caught up by the Zips' Corvin Amos. Brown scored two touchdowns in Iowa's 57-21 victory. Zach Boyden-Holmes/The Daily Iowan

Akron managed just 67 yards rushing, but the Zips passed for 296 against an Iowa secondary that was in obvious need of some fine-tuning. Ferentz said the situation will be addressed in the coming week before Iowa travels to Miami of Ohio.

Ferentz credited Iowa's dominating performance against the Zips to preparation.

"We're pleased to get the win today," he said. "We were ready to play at kickoff."

With the victory, the Hawkeyes begin looking ahead to what could be a tough road trip to Miami next weekend. Iowa will be the first Big Ten team to visit the RedHawks, and the school has been heavily advertising the appearance. It may also help that the Hawkeyes handed Miami a 44-19 thrashing in Kinnick Stadium last season.

"We've got to prepare for the Miami game," Ferentz said. "They've been hyping this game up for quite some time, and it's going to be a wild environment where we have to come prepared to play."

RIGHT:

Iowa defensive back D. J. Johnson attempts to take the ball away from Akron receiver Jamie Goodwin. Zach Boyden-Holmes/The Daily Iowan

ABOVE:
Iowa linebacker Fred Barr, left, and lineman Matt Roth take down Akron quarterback Nick Sparks. Zach Boyden-Holmes/The Daily Iowan

RIGHT:
Hawkeyes defender D. J. Johnson tries to deflect a Jamie Goodwin reception. Goodwin eventually came down with the ball and a 31-yard touchdown reception. Ben Plank/The Daily Iowan

LEFT:
Iowa defensive back Derek Pagel tackles Akron's Brandon Payne. Payne gained only 32 yards on seven carries. Ben Plank/The Daily Iowan

"*I WAS SURPRISED THAT [IOWA] SCORED AS MUCH AS THEY DID, BUT I WASN'T SURPRISED THAT THEY CAME OUT RIPPING AND ROARING.*"
—AKRON COACH LEE OWENS

Zach Boyden-Holmes/The Daily Iowan

SATURDAY, SEPTEMBER 7, 2002
IOWA HAWKEYES 29 AT MIAMI RED HAWKS 24

REDSCARE

Hawks fight off Miami 29-24 on the road

BY TODD BROMMELKAMP
DAILY IOWAN ASSISTANT SPORTS EDITOR

OXFORD, Ohio— The Iowa Hawkeyes did not play a perfect game against Miami University, but they did enough to escape with a 29-24 victory.

Iowa was penalized six times for 74 yards, fumbled on a punt return for the second straight week, and struggled at times against the inspired RedHawks, but escaped Oxford with a victory and plenty of areas to work on heading in to next weekend's highly anticipated showdown with Iowa State.

"We knew this was going to be a challenge," Iowa coach Kirk Ferentz said. "We feel fortunate to get out of here with a victory."

A relentless RedHawk squad picked away at the Hawkeyes all day, eventually taking a 17-16 lead in the third quarter when Cal Murray recovered a teammate's fumble in the end zone for the go-ahead score.

But the Hawkeyes regrouped behind a 12-yard run from backup running back Jermelle Lewis and a 48-yard

BELOW: Hawkeyes running back Jermelle Lewis pushes back defenders on his way to the end zone. Lewis ran 12 yards to give Iowa a 22-17 third-quarter lead. Zach Boyden-Holmes/The Daily Iowan

ABOVE: *Hawkeyes head coach Kirk Ferentz yells out instructions during Iowa's 29-24 win over Miami.*
Zach Boyden-Holmes/The Daily Iowan

touchdown pass from Brad Banks to C. J. Jones provided enough breathing room to strangle any hopes of a Miami upset.

"We were out of answers," Ferentz said. "We just started letting it fly."

The Hawkeyes started and finished strong but did not turn in the all-around effort Ferentz would have liked to have seen.

"We started out with a nice drive and ended with one, but in between we had some struggles," he said.

Iowa began the game pinned on the one-yard line by a pooch punt after holding the RedHawks on their first possession. Quarterback Brad Banks led the Hawkeyes on a 99-yard, 13-play scoring drive that culminated in a four-yard Fred Russell touchdown run.

Russell finished the day with 150 yards and one touchdown on 32 carries, the second week in a row the junior rushed for more than 100 yards. He credited his performance to Iowa's offensive line, which for the second straight week overpowered and wore down its opposition.

"Running behind those guys today, I didn't have to make anybody miss," Russell said. "They did a great job."

Miami utilized a strong passing attack from Ben Roethlisberger to keep the Iowa defense on its toes most of the day. Roethlisberger finished the day 33 of 51 with 343 yards passing and three touchdowns.

BELOW: *C. J. Jones and teammates celebrate in the end zone after Jones's 48-yard touchdown reception in the fourth quarter.*
Zach Boyden-Holmes/The Daily Iowan

	1st	2nd	3rd	4th	Final
IOWA	**7**	**6**	**9**	**7**	**29**
MIAMI (OH)	**0**	**10**	**7**	**7**	**24**

SCORING SUMMARY

QTR	TEAM	PLAY		TIME
1st	**HAWKEYES**	TD	Russell 4-yd. run (Kaeding kick)	5:50
2nd	**REDHAWKS**	FG	Parseghian 36-yd.	14:44
2nd	**HAWKEYES**	FG	Kaeding 37-yd.	9:55
2nd	**REDHAWKS**	TD	Larkin 27-yd. pass from Roethlisberger (Parseghian kick)	5:44
2nd	**HAWKEYES**	FG	Kaeding 27-yd.	1:02
3rd	**HAWKEYES**	FG	Kaeding 49-yd.	6:36
3rd	**REDHAWKS**	TD	Murray 0-yd. offensive fumble return (Parseghian kick)	3:01
3rd	**HAWKEYES**	TD	Lewis 12-yd. run (Failed 2-pt. pass)	1:30
4th	**HAWKEYES**	TD	Jones 48-yd. pass from Banks (Kaeding kick)	11:44
4th	**REDHAWKS**	TD	Branch 24-yd. pass from Roethlisberger (Parseghian kick)	4:54

———— OFFENSE ————

HAWKEYES

PASSING	ATT	COMP	YDS	INT	TD
Roethlisberger	51	33	343	1	2

RECEIVING	CATCHES	YDS	TD
Larkin	7	83	1
Branch	6	70	1
Kirkpatrick	6	62	0
Henderson	4	37	0
Iriti	3	37	0
Brandt	3	27	0
Tillitz	2	7	0
Smith	1	12	0
Clemens	1	8	0

RUSHING	RUSHES	YDS	TD
Murray	6	18	0
Clemens	5	12	0
Smith	1	7	0
Roethlisberger	5	-23	0

RED HAWKS

PASSING	ATT	COMP	YDS	INT	TD
Banks	27	18	256	0	1

RECEIVING	CATCHES	YDS	TD
Brown	5	115	0
Hinkel	4	31	0
Jones	3	64	1
Solomon	3	35	0
Clark	3	11	0

RUSHING	RUSHES	YDS	TD
Russell	32	150	1
Lewis	3	21	1
Cervantes	2	18	0
Banks	2	2	0

"He's a tremendous football player," Ferentz said. "He's tough to defend and he throws the ball around and really does a nice job."

Roethlisberger connected with Jason Branch for a 24-yard touchdown strike with just under five minutes remaining in the game, but the RedHawks failed to recover an onside kick.

Iowa also fielded a strong passing game, with Banks completing 18 of 27 attempts for one touchdown, a 48-yard score to C. J. Jones that extended Iowa's lead to 29-17. Maurice Brown led the Hawkeyes with 115 yards on five receptions.

"Our defense rose to the occasion many times...but we just didn't overcome enough adversity today," Miami coach Terry Hoeppner said.

Kicker Nate Kaeding helped to keep Iowa in the game, connecting on all three of his field goal attempts, including a 49-yarder which tied his career high.

"I know I have to be ready to come in and play well and today I was able to get the ball to go through [the uprights]," Kaeding said.

RIGHT:
Iowa's Colin Cole closes in on RedHawks quarterback Ben Roethlisberger. Roethlisberger was sacked four times on the afternoon. Zach Boyden-Holmes/The Daily Iowan

BELOW:
Tight end Dallas Clark breaks a tackle during Iowa's win over Miami. Clark had three receptions for 11 yards. Zach Boyden-Holmes/The Daily Iowan

" WE KNEW THIS WAS GOING TO BE A CHALLENGE. WE FEEL
FORTUNATE TO GET OUT OF HERE WITH A VICTORY.
—IOWA COACH KIRK FERENTZ "

Miami's Jason Branch dives for the ball while Iowa's D. J. Johnson defends. Branch caught six passes for 70 yards and a touchdown. Zach Boyden-Holmes/The Daily Iowan

Iowa running back Fred Russell evades a RedHawk defender. Russell finished with 150 yards rushing on 32 attempts. Zach Boyden-Holmes/The Daily Iowan

95

NATE KAEDING

BY BRIAN TRIPLETT, DAILY IOWAN REPORTER

Nate Kaeding is kicking himself.

Into the record books, that is.

The Hawkeyes' placekicker has been breaking so many records that some of the only records left to break are his own.

Whether he is setting a new milestone or one of his streaks is ending, it seems as though a majority of the time Penn State has something to do with it.

Against Penn State on Sept. 28, Kaeding kicked in his 13th consecutive field goal. That broke his previous school mark of 11, which was put to rest in 2001 against the Nittany Lions.

Penn State also ended another streak of Kaeding's when his school PAT record ended at 60 after his second-quarter extra point attempt was blocked in this season's game in Happy Valley. "I didn't really worry about that," said Kaeding, who is the nation's 14th leading scorer this season. "That was a good play on the Penn State guy's part. We were just disappointed because we didn't score the point out there."

This doesn't mean that Penn State has always gotten the best of Kaeding. In his freshman season, he racked up four field goals and two PATs in a 26-23 overtime victory against the Nittany Lions, earning him Big Ten special teams Player of the Week honors. His 14 kicking points that game tied a school record, which he would go on to break the following season against Kent State when he scored 15 points on three field goals and six PATs.

On top of that, in this year's game against a No. 12-ranked Penn State team, he booted field goals of 47 and 55 yards and held part of the Big Ten special teams Player of the Week honors once again. His 55-yarder tied for the third longest in Iowa history and gave the Hawkeyes a momentum-building 26-7 lead as time expired in the first half.

Iowa coach Kirk Ferentz said he would not have opted for the field goal had the Hawkeyes been back much farther, but he does have a lot of trust in his kicker.

"He's not fragile at all," Ferentz said. "He's like a bona fide football player. I think that's a big part of his success."

CLASS: JR.

AGE: 20

HOMETOWN: CORALVILLE, IA

Kaeding: Curtis Lehmkuh/The Daily Iowan

PLACE KICKER

Kaeding claims, however, that his range is from about 60 to 65 yards, and he has hit 70-yarders with the help of the wind.

"I'm just worried about helping out this football team and helping it win games," Kaeding said. "We got something awesome going on right now this year."

Success has always been a big part of Kaeding's athletics career, even in his high school days.

He grew up in Coralville and attended Iowa City West High School, where he holds every kicking and punting record. His football team won state championships his junior and senior years and had a record of 26-0.

In his senior year at West, Kaeding started on the state champion basketball team and also kicked in his soccer team's final point of a shootout for a victory in the state championship game.

If anyone knows as much about Kaeding's success as he does, it's his parents.

Larry and Terry Kaeding have attended every one of Nate's collegiate games, home and away, but one. The game they did not attend happened to be the one against Penn State in 2000 when Kaeding tied the 14-point kicking record and earned Big Ten special teams Player of the Week honors. His mother claimed she and her husband will never miss another game.

"His determination is one thing we've noticed since the time he was very young," said Nate's mother, Terry. "His leadership abilities were always very evident, and he always liked being the center of attention."

As a kicker, Kaeding often is the center of attention. In last year's Alamo Bowl against Texas Tech, all eyes were on Kaeding as he kicked in a 47-yard field goal with 44 seconds remaining to give the Hawkeyes a 19-16 victory. The field goal was Kaeding's fourth of the game, setting the Iowa bowl game record.

If this production continues, Kaeding will no doubt surpass Rob Houghtlin's record of 290 career points to become the most prolific scorer in Iowa football history.

There are still some records for Kaeding to break and still some time to break them.

The longest field goal in Iowa football history is 58 yards, set by Tim Douglas in 1998.

With a strong leg and a little help from the wind, maybe Kaeding could add one more record to his book.

No pros? Rivalry key to Iowa state pride

BY TODD BROMMELKAMP
DAILY IOWAN ASSISTANT SPORTS EDITOR

I do an extensive amount of traveling for someone with no social life and very little money, and more often than not, when folks hear of my locale, they have questions about Iowa.

I sometimes struggle to explain that there is more to this fair state than fields of corn and soybeans between two rivers. But when among sports fans, the query I field most often involves what Iowans do to quench our thirst for action. Iowa, these astute observers usually inform me, has no major-league franchises.

But we do have Iowa and Iowa State.

It's like our Super Bowl, minus John Madden and the washed-up pop stars. If only Tom Arnold could lip-synch some off-key caterwauling at halftime—something along the lines of his ex-wife—our state would be in business.

And just like the real Super Bowl, the game itself takes a back seat to the pomp and circumstance surrounding it. Ticket prices get spiked, and no one complains. Fans from both sides take shots at one another. Fans from both sides take shots with one another. But mostly they take them at one another.

Take for instance the Internet, which has helped this rivalry reach epic proportions of bad taste. Cyclone fans are clowns rather than 'Clones, and Iowa State is Moo U. or Silo U. To those in Ames, it's not Hawks but Squawks, and the official name of our fine institution is Eastern Iowa University. Can you imagine these people drinking until Saturday's 5 p.m. kickoff at Kinnick Stadium?

Tom Vilsack, who will be in attendance attempting to be roundly booed during athletics events at all three regents schools, may have to put the state's kindergarten teachers on a state of high alert to deal with the slurs that will be slurred about.

"Iowa State fans eat paste."

"The Hawkeyes are stinky pants."

Heck, that's already a step in the right direction over the venom being spewed back and forth currently. Iowa State fans still have an unsettling obsession with Hayden Fry, and their Hawkeye brethren are equally willing to live in the past as they recount the glory days of 15 victories in a row over the "ketchup and mustard." There may be a Bush in the White House, but the last time anyone checked this was 2002, not 1992.

Photos by Zach Boyden-Holmes/The Daily Iowan

"*FANS FROM BOTH SIDES TAKE SHOTS AT ONE ANOTHER. FANS FROM BOTH SIDES TAKE SHOTS WITH ONE ANOTHER. BUT MOSTLY THEY TAKE THEM AT ONE ANOTHER.*"

BELOW: *Students watch the Hawkeyes take the field before the Sept. 14, 2002 matchup between the Hawkeyes and Cyclones.* Ben Plank/The Daily Iowan

Both sides spend so much time preoccupied with living in the last century that for the most part they have forgotten there will be one helluva football game played this weekend. For the first time in many, many moons, both the Hawkeyes and Cyclones are fielding respectable teams—last season is apparently still open to debate on both sides. Seneca Wallace and Brad Banks are the most exciting quarterbacks to ever meet head to head in the series and should provide plenty of fireworks.

Perhaps most important, however, is that fans of both teams "suck" and are "jerks."

Who needs professional sports when you've got this?

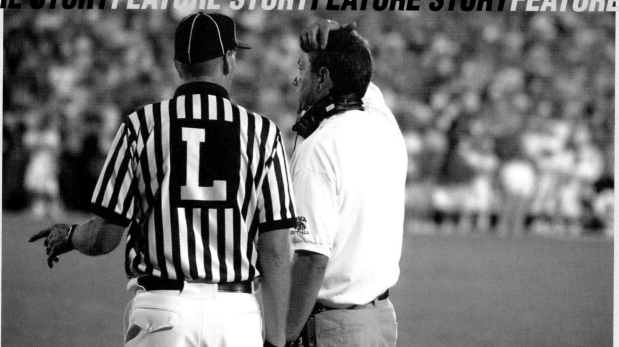

ABOVE:

Hawkeyes head coach Kirk Ferentz discusses a questionable call with an official during Iowa State's 36-31 win over Iowa on Sept. 14. Zach Boyden-Holmes/The Daily Iowan

RIGHT:

Fans react to Iowa quarterback Brad Banks's second fumble of the game as Iowa State dismantles what was a 24-7 Hawkeye lead at halftime. Zach Boyden-Holmes/The Daily Iowan

LEFT:

University of Iowa senior Chris "Joker" Lavens cheers on the Hawkeyes by slamming the side of the retaining wall in the student section. Ben Plank/The Daily Iowan

SATURDAY, SEPTEMBER 14, 2002
IOWA STATE CYCLONES 36 AT IOWA HAWKEYES 31

STATE OF SHOCK

Cyclones take fifth straight behind big second half

BY TODD BROMMELKAMP
DAILY IOWAN ASSISTANT SPORTS EDITOR

Facing a 24-7 halftime deficit, Iowa State coach Dan McCarney told his players that if they were going to get beaten he wanted them to go down swinging. They certainly came out swinging in the second half of the Cyclones' 36-31 victory over Iowa, but it was the Hawkeyes who delivered their own knockout punch.

Quarterback Seneca Wallace led the Cyclones on a 75-yard drive to begin the second half, which ended with Wallace keeping the ball on a five-yard run to pull Iowa State within 14 points. On Iowa's subsequent two possessions quarterback Brad Banks fumbled twice, both of which led to key Iowa State scores.

BELOW: Iowa State defenders bring down Iowa quarterback Brad Banks. Banks was sacked three times in the game.
Ben Plank/The Daily Iowan

ABOVE:
Hawkeyes tight end Erik Jensen pulls away from a Cyclones defender. Jensen gained 25 yards on the play, his only reception of the game. Zach Boyden-Holmes/The Daily Iowan

Banks fumbled near midfield on Iowa's first drive of the second half, giving the Cyclones the ball on the Iowa 33-yard line. It took Wallace just five plays to find Jamaul Montgomery in the back of the end zone for a seven-yard touchdown pass. After the ensuing kickoff and with Iowa pushing the ball upfield, Banks fumbled again when sacked by Iowa State's Tim TeBrink at the 20-yard line. Fullback Joe Woodley eventually pushed the ball across the goal line from the one-yard line to give the Cyclones their first lead of the game, 28-24.

Iowa State also recorded a safety after Jermelle Lewis botched the kickoff, forcing Iowa to start the drive on their own five. Aaron Greving hesitated on a run up the middle and was brought down on the goal line by Jeremy Loyd for two points, extending Iowa State's lead to six points.

"They won the most important half of the game," Iowa coach Kirk Ferentz said.

It was a far cry from the game's first half, which saw the Hawkeyes hold Iowa State to just 21 yards rushing

BELOW: *Iowa running back Jermelle Lewis tries to escape the grasp of an Iowa State defender. Lewis gained 20 yards on five carries and scored a touchdown.* Ben Plank/The Daily Iowan

	1st	2nd	3rd	4th	Final
IOWA STATE	7	0	23	6	36
IOWA	7	17	0	7	31

SCORING SUMMARY

QTR	TEAM	PLAY		TIME
1st	**HAWKEYES**	TD	Russell 46-yd. run (Kaeding kick)	14:00
1st	**CYCLONES**	TD	Rutland 6-yd. run (Benike kick)	7:51
2nd	**HAWKEYES**	FG	Kaeding 40-yd.	10:34
2nd	**HAWKEYES**	TD	Brown 50-yd. pass from Banks (Kaeding kick)	9:17
2nd	**HAWKEYES**	TD	Lewis 10-yd. run (Kaeding kick)	2:47
3rd	**CYCLONES**	TD	Wallace 5-yd. run (Benike kick)	10:58
3rd	**CYCLONES**	TD	Montgomery 7-yd. pass from Wallace (Benike kick)	7:24
3rd	**CYCLONES**	TD	Woodley 1-yd. run (Benike kick)	4:31
3rd	**CYCLONES**	ST	Jeremy Loyd safety	4:16
4th	**CYCLONES**	FG	Benike 36-yd.	5:19
4th	**CYCLONES**	FG	Benike 38-yd.	4:08
4th	**HAWKEYES**	TD	Brown 24-yd. pass from Banks (Kaeding kick)	1:23

——— OFFENSE ———

CYCLONES

PASSING	ATT	COMP	YDS	INT	TD
Wallace	37	23	361	1	1

RECEIVING	CATCHES	YDS	TD
Whitver	8	132	0
Danielsen	5	131	0
Montgomery	4	36	1
Young	3	47	0
Rutland	3	15	0

RUSHING	RUSHES	YDS	TD
Rutland	21	50	1
Wallace	12	30	1
Wagner	4	7	0
Woodley	1	1	1
Danielsen	1	-3	0

HAWKEYES

PASSING	ATT	COMP	YDS	INT	TD
Banks	21	12	178	0	2

RECEIVING	CATCHES	YDS	TD
Brown	4	89	2
Jones	3	30	0
Hinkel	2	21	0
Solomon	2	13	0
Jensen	1	25	0

RUSHING	RUSHES	YDS	TD
Russell	17	151	1
Greving	9	32	0
Lewis	5	19	1
Banks	9	11	0
Cervantes	2	9	0

and one score. Fred Russell compiled 133 of his 139 yards in the first half before leaving the game early in the second half due to injury. He scored the game's first touchdown on Iowa's opening possession when he broke a 46-yard run, which electrified the sellout crowd of 70,397 and set the tone for the game's first half.

"We got taken to the woodshed in the first half," McCarney said. "They just completely beat us in every way.

"We looked like a scout team."

With the game tied at seven, Iowa's Nate Kaeding connected on a 40-yard field goal to give Iowa a 10-7 lead. Maurice Brown and Jermelle Lewis each scored before the half to give Iowa a 24-7 halftime advantage. Brown hauled in a 50-yard pass from Banks with 9:17 remaining and Lewis pounded out a 10-yard touchdown on the ground at the 2:47 mark.

The win marks Iowa State's fifth straight over the Hawkeyes dating back to a 27-9 victory in 1998 at Kinnick Stadium.

"It's been five tough years," said Iowa defensive back Derek Pagel. "Every year you think you're going to beat them...and you don't."

BELOW: Hawkeyes quarterback Brad Banks fumbles the ball. Zach Boyden-Holmes/The Daily Iowan

Iowa State added a pair of crucial field goals by Adam Benike in the fourth quarter, which extended the lead to 36-24. It was enough cushioning to offset a 20-yard touchdown pass to Brown from Banks with 1:23 remaining in the game. Attempts to recover an onside kick by the Hawkeyes failed, allowing the Cyclones run down the clock and let time expire.

Wallace finished the game with 361 yards passing on 37 attempts, 23 of which were completions, setting a new career high. It was also the most yards allowed through the air by Iowa yet this season and negated the fact Iowa held the Cyclones to just 85 yards rushing on the day.

"I give it up to Seneca Wallace, he's a great athlete," said Iowa's Colin Cole.

Cole finished second on the team behind Pagel and Kevin Worthy in tackles with nine, including three for a loss. Pagel and Worthy finished with 11 stops each.

Banks threw for 178 yards on 12-of-21 passing, but his two fumbles are what will be remembered as Iowa prepares to host Utah State next weekend.

"I had a lot of mistakes out there," Banks said. "I take a whole lot of [the blame]."

While turnovers certainly helped aid Iowa State, Ferentz gave credit to Iowa State for entering a hostile environment and pulling out a come-from-behind victory. The game reminded many observers of Iowa State's 38-31 loss to Florida State in the Eddie Robinson Classic Aug. 24 with one notable exception—the outcome.

"I don't like to compare games; I don't see how you can," McCarney said. "But when you're down like that and come back to win, it's really something special."

BELOW:
Hawkeyes defenders take down Cyclones receiver Jack Whitver. Whitver caught eight passes for 132 yards. Ben Plank/The Daily Iowan

❝ *IT'S BEEN A TOUGH FIVE YEARS. EVERY YEAR YOU THINK YOU'RE GOING TO BEAT THEM ... AND YOU DON'T.* ❞

—IOWA SENIOR DEFENSIVE BACK
DEREK PAGEL

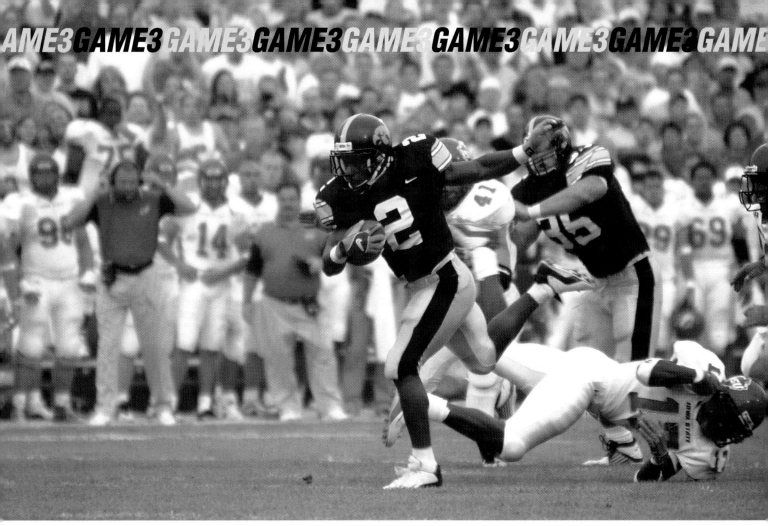

LEFT:
Hawkeyes linebacker Kevin Worthy puts a hit on Cyclones quarterback Seneca Wallace in the end zone. Zach Boyden-Holmes/The Daily Iowan

ABOVE: *Iowa running back Fred Russell blows past Cyclones defenders. Brown gained 148 yards on 36 carries.* Zach Boyden-Holmes/The Daily Iowan

BELOW: *Iowa receiver Maurice Brown dives into the end zone to bring the Hawkeyes within five with 1:23 remaining.* Zach Boyden-Holmes/The Daily Iowan

Zach Boyden-Holmes/The Daily Iowan

UTAH STATE AGGIES 7 AT IOWA HAWKEYES 48

IOWA TOPS UTAH STATE, 48-7

Hawks avoid repeat of second-half meltdown, Lewis rushes for 109 yards

BY TODD BROMMELKAMP
DAILY IOWAN ASSISTANT SPORTS EDITOR

The halftime score was the same, but the end result was not.

Behind 518 yards of total offense, Iowa routed visiting Utah State, 48-7, in Kinnick Stadium in the team's final tune-up before Big Ten play begins.

Just one week after allowing Iowa State to rally from a 24-7 halftime deficit, the Hawkeyes faced a similar situation against the Aggies when they found themselves staring at the same 24-7 score heading in to the locker rooms.

"I'm sure it was on a lot of people's minds," said kicker Nate Kaeding, who connected on field goal attempts of 35 and 51 yards.

Unlike in last week's contest, the Hawkeyes kept their composure leaving the locker room, putting 24 third-quarter points on the board to put the game well out of the Aggies' reach.

ABOVE:
Iowa defensive tackle Colin Cole takes down Utah State quarterback Jeff Crosbie during the Hawkeyes' 48-7 romp over the Aggies. Curtis Lehmkuhl/The Daily Iowan

ABOVE:
Hawkeyes tight end Dallas Clark runs away from Aggies defenders. Clark led Iowa with 67 receiving yards on five catches.
Curtis Lehmkuhl/The Daily Iowan

"This was a good old-fashioned butt whippin'," Utah State coach Mick Dennehy said. "We knew what they were going to do, when they were going to do it, and had a hell of a hard time stopping them."

Jermelle Lewis, who saw his workload increase due to injuries to running backs Aaron Greving and Fred Russell, started Iowa off on the right foot in the third quarter with his only rushing touchdown of the day. Lewis broke a 75-yard run around the right end to extend Iowa's lead to 31-7 and erase any momentum the Aggies hoped to have gained.

Lewis finished the day with a career-high 109 yards on nine carries to lead the Hawkeyes, who piled up exactly 300 rushing yards. Quarterback Brad Banks added 65 yards on seven attempts while Greving and Marcus Schnoor each added 48 and 44 yards, respectively.

Lewis's touchdown was Iowa's only offensive score of the second half. Iowa's remaining two touchdowns came on special teams and defense. Mike Follett fell on a blocked punt by Sean Considine in the end zone to extend Iowa's lead to 38-7, and defensive lineman Jared Clauss covered up a fumble in the end zone for Iowa's final score of the game with 3:34 remaining in the third quarter.

BELOW:

Hawkeyes quarterback Brad Banks twists past the Aggies' defense. Banks ran for 65 yards on seven carries to go along with 185 passing yards. Lucas Underwood/The Daily Iowan

THIS WAS A GOOD OLD-FASHIONED BUTT WHIPPIN'. WE KNEW WHAT THEY WERE GOING TO DO, WHEN THEY WERE GOING TO DO IT, AND HAD A HELL OF A HARD TIME STOPPING THEM.

—Utah State head coach Mick Dennehy

	1st	2nd	3rd	4th	Final
UTAH STATE	0	7	0	0	7
IOWA	14	10	24	0	48

SCORING SUMMARY

QTR	TEAM	PLAY		TIME
1st	**HAWKEYES**	TD	Jones 12-yd. pass from Banks (Kaeding kick)	8:45
1st	**HAWKEYES**	TD	Cervantes 1-yd. run (Kaeding kick)	3:18
2nd	**HAWKEYES**	TD	Banks 1-yd. run (Kaeding kick)	11:04
2nd	**AGGIES**	TD	Robinson 25-yd. run (Kidman kick)	6:12
2nd	**HAWKEYES**	FG	Kaeding 35-yd.	3:11
3rd	**HAWKEYES**	TD	Lewis 75-yd. run (Kaeding kick)	10:42
3rd	**HAWKEYES**	TD	Follett 0-yd. blocked punt return.	9:33
3rd	**HAWKEYES**	FG	Kaeding 51-yd.	4:37
3rd	**HAWKEYES**	TD	Clauss 0-yd. defensive fumble return (Kaeding kick)	1:30

———— OFFENSE ————

AGGIES

PASSING	ATT	COMP	YDS	INT	TD
Fuentes	36	21	214	0	0
Cox	3	3	9	0	0
Crosbie	2	0	0	0	0

RECEIVING	CATCHES	YDS	TD
Curtis	7	51	0
Samuel	5	46	0
Coleman	4	58	0
Fiefia	3	9	0
Watson	2	22	0
Robinson	1	13	0
Jeffery	1	13	0
Poppinga	1	11	0

RUSHING	RUSHES	YDS	TD
Robinson	3	30	1
Samuel	7	15	0
Watson	1	4	0
Cox	2	0	0
Fiefia	2	-1	0
Crosbie	2	-12	0
Fuentes	2	-15	0

HAWKEYES

PASSING	ATT	COMP	YDS	INT	TD
Banks	29	15	185	0	1
Chandler	4	2	33	0	0

RECEIVING	CATCHES	YDS	TD
Clark	5	67	0
Brown	4	28	0
Solomon	2	50	0
Ochoa	2	33	0
Hinkel	2	29	0
Jones	1	12	1
Greving	1	-1	0

RUSHING	RUSHES	YDS	TD
Lewis	9	109	1
Banks	7	65	1
Greving	12	48	0
Schnoor	12	44	0
Cervantes	4	28	1
Mickens	3	4	0
Chandler	1	3	0
Sherlock	1	-1	0

"We were a little ragged in some areas that need to be cleaned up, but overall I thought the guys did well," Iowa coach Kirk Ferentz said.

"We scored on defense and special teams, which is something we haven't done this year."

Utah State managed just 244 yards of offense against the Hawkeyes, including just 21 yards on the ground against the nation's seventh best rush defense. Iowa entered the game allowing just 55 yards per game on the ground. Running back Roger Robinson scored the Aggies' only touchdown of the day on a 25-yard run midway through the second quarter.

Iowa grabbed momentum in the game early, scoring the first 21 points of the game before Robinson's touchdown. Banks hit C. J. Jones with a 12-yard scoring strike on Iowa's first possession of the game before the Hawkeyes added rushing touchdowns of one yard by fullback Edgar Cervantes and Banks.

The victory gives the Hawkeyes some much-needed confidence heading in to next weekend's Big Ten opener against undefeated Penn State in Happy Valley. Iowa has won its last two meetings against the Lions.

"We're definitely going to have to bring our 'A' game," tight end Dallas Clark said.

BELOW: Hawkeyes wide receiver Clinton Solomon heads downfield during his 43-yard reception in the second quarter.
Curtis Lehmkuhl/The Daily Iowan

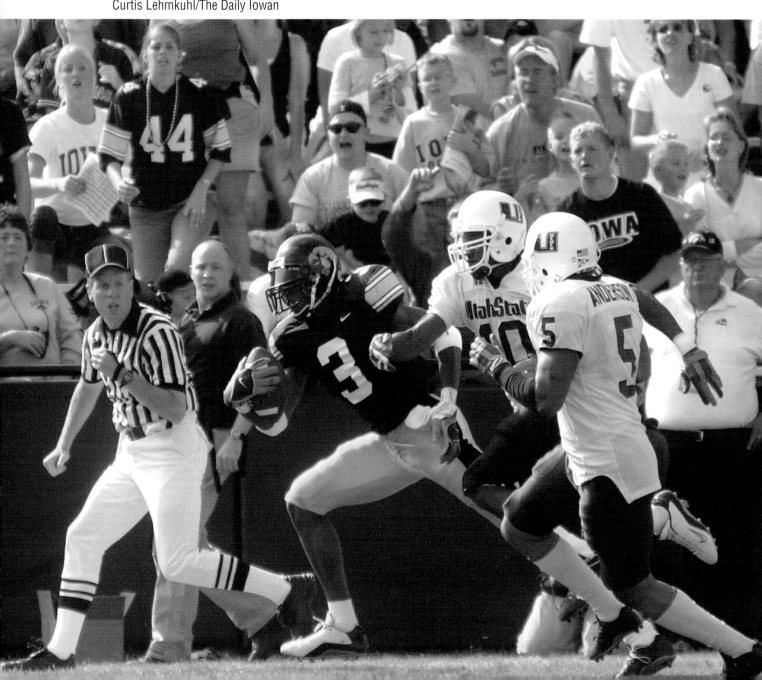

Iowa cheerleaders animate the crowd during the Hawkeyes' victory over the Aggies. Lucas Underwood/The Daily Iowan

BELOW:

Utah State quarterback Jeff Crosbie releases the ball under pressure from Iowa defensive tackle O. J. Payne. Curtis Lehmkuhl/The Daily Iowan

ABOVE:
Iowa right end Howard Hodges takes down the Utah State quarterback. Lucas Underwood/The Daily Iowan

LEFT:
Iowa receiver Maurice Brown is brought down by a Utah State defender. Brown caught four passes for 28 yards. Lucas Underwood/The Daily Iowan

CLASS: SO.

JERMELLE LEWIS 29

BY BRIAN TRIPLETT, DAILY IOWAN REPORTER

Anything Jermelle Lewis does is for the team. Just ask two of the people who know him best, his coach and his mother, and that's what they'll say.

The sophomore running back has been given a few opportunities this season to show what he can do for the Hawkeyes, but mostly he has been waiting patiently on the sidelines for his turn.

That opportunity could come on Saturday with yet another twist in the running back situation.

Last season, starting running back Ladell Betts went down, and backup Aaron Greving got a chance to shine in the Alamo Bowl. This year, Greving got hurt, so Lewis and Fred Russell showed what they could do.

"I gotta do what I gotta do for the team," he said. "If it means for me to step up and start, then I'm gonna have to do that."

Although Lewis is enjoying a successful 2002 season, the road to that success has not been paved for the Connecticut native.

Lewis came to Iowa in 2000 and redshirted his freshman season. Like a typical freshman, he did what he needed to do to get by with his schoolwork, but then things took a turn for the worse. In the fall of Lewis's sophomore year, his scholarship was taken away because of academic struggles.

"It was like an empty feeling," Lewis said. "I don't want to go back there any more."

Lewis was away from football for the 2001 season, but with encourage-

Ben Plank/The Daily Iowan

AGE: 20

HOMETOWN: BLOOMFIELD, CT

RUNNING BACK

ment from those surrounding him, Lewis overcame his struggles and got his grades back where they needed to be. He began playing football again for the Hawkeyes in the spring of 2002 and regained his scholarship.

"It looked kind of dark for a minute, but my teammates stuck by me 100 percent," Lewis said. "Coach Ferentz stuck by me 100 percent, like we're gonna make it through this."

Offensive lineman Robert Gallery is one of those teammates that stuck by Lewis's side.

"It's something that we've all been through … those down times," Gallery said. "I just took him aside and told him things are gonna get better because I know he's a great worker."

Lewis rushed for 124 yards and two touchdowns against Akron in the season opener behind Russell, who rushed for 170 yards. He also had breakout games against Utah St., rushing for 109 yards, including Iowa's longest run from scrimmage this season—a 75-yard touchdown—and against Michigan, where he repeated his 109-yard output and reached the end zone on two occasions.

"He's been fantastic," said coach Kirk Ferentz of Lewis. "He's an aggressive runner. He wants to fight for that extra yard."

Lewis has known all about fighting for those extra yards ever since his days of playing tackle football on the snowy streets of Connecticut.

"We'd let the snowplow come by and build up all the snow on the sides. Then we'd get in the streets and play football … sideline crack and everything. We loved football."

In high school, Lewis starred all four years for Bloomfield and was part of three state champion squads. He was named first-team All-State his junior and senior years, racking up nearly 4,000 yards and 54 touchdowns.

Along with his strong football game, Lewis also has a strong character. His mother told a story of how one of Jermelle's teammates in high school was struggling to make it, so Jermelle took him aside and asked him if he was trying the absolute best he could. When his teammate responded yes, Jermelle gave him a pep talk, saying that was all anyone could ask for.

"Jermelle didn't tell me this," said his mother Cathy Andrews. "The mother of his teammate told me. That's just the way Jermelle is."

Although competition has been strong between the Iowa running backs, Lewis says there are no hard feelings between him and Russell.

"We're like brothers back there," Lewis said. "He points out my mistakes. I point out his mistakes. We try to help each other to be the best backs in the Big Ten."

"I guess everybody says Fred's a slasher, a quicker back than I am," said Lewis when asked to compare the two. "I could never tell anybody how I run." Lewis's performance on the field with have to do the talking.

57

RIGHT:

Hawkeye offensive linemen(from left) David Porter, Andy Lightfoot, Bruce Nelson and Eric Steinbach prepare for a play against Minnesota. Ben Plank/The Daily Iowan

FRIDAY, OCTOBER 4, 2002

After long wait,
Iowa Hawkeyes offensive line finally hits stride

Behind the numbers of running backs and quarterbacks, the members of the veteran line drive toward being the best five in the Big Ten

BY DONOVAN BURBA
DAILY IOWAN REPORTER

Here's a riddle: What local group has an average height and weight of 6'6" and 295 pounds, respectively? No, not the lunchtime crowd at Denny's, but good guess. The Hawkeyes' offensive line fits that physical bill, making it perhaps the most formidable such unit in the Big Ten. The members are fast, strong, and unlike those midday munchers, they block more than just the sun.

Offensive linemen are the only players in football who don't have official stats. Oh sure, some teams keep track of "pancakes," a glorified term for "really good block," but there's no official statistical standard for a pancake (or any other breakfast food, for that matter). The best measure of an offensive line are the statistics of the offensive "skill" players, particularly the quarterback and running backs. Even the quickest glance at Iowa's numbers shows that the Hawkeyes' line is in an elite class.

On the ground, the Hawkeyes have accumulated 1,295 rushing yards, averaging 5.8 yards per carry and 259 per game—on top in the Big Ten in all three categories. It is a testament to the line that Iowa has had such success without preseason starting running back Aaron Greving, who has played sparingly while he recovers from an ankle injury. Fred Russell, Greving's replacement, third in the nation in yards per game with 153.2, is certainly skilled, with the ability to hit holes with lightning-quick speed. But consider this: Iowa has had a 100-yard rusher in each of its last eight games. Impressive, but even more amazing when one considers that four different backs contributed to that streak (Russell, Greving, Jermelle Lewis, and Ladell Betts). The one constant in all eight games? The offensive line.

"We feel good about [the streak]," said senior center Bruce Nelson. "We struggled in the past with having a solid running game, and now we're really getting the ball moving on the ground, and that's certainly a feather in our hat."

Russell, for his part, isn't complaining either.

"[Running behind the line] makes things a lot easier for me," he said. "I have a lot of confidence in the guys, and I hope they have the confidence in me."

Quarterback Brad Banks is another beneficiary of the Great Wall of Iowa. Banks, considered by many to be impatient in the pocket, is able to drop back without worrying about the defensive rush. The line has allowed only five sacks all year, and Banks, with more time to make accurate reads and throws, has completed nearly 60 percent of his passes.

Character, as much as size, dictates how successful a line will be, and one would be hard-pressed to find a unit with more character than the Hawkeyes' O-line. Four starters are seniors, including David Porter, who is playing his fifth season for Iowa. The fifth member, junior Robert Gallery, started all 12 games last year after moving from tight end in 2000. Even though Iowa is now ranked in the top 25 nationally, the veterans still have memories of leaner days.

BELOW: Iowa's offensive line prepares for the snap Nov. 16 at Minnesota. Ben Plank/The Daily Iowan

"We understand how rough things can be, and now we're understanding how good things can be," said Nelson, who suffered through the Hawkeyes' 1999-00 seasons, in which they went a combined 4-19. "We don't want anybody to get too high or to get too low, so we just try to stay in that steady and level path."

While that path may have been a little rougher than anyone in the Iowa program would have liked, coach Kirk Ferentz knew that it was just a matter of time before the offensive line lived up to its potential.

"Going into the season last year, we hoped they'd hit stride, and I think they did," he said. "They've really been resilient and persevered through some rough times, and I think they're enjoying where they're sitting right now."

While the line may have hit stride last year, paving the way for Betts to run for more than 1,000 yards, it suffered one major stumble—against Purdue. The Boilermakers completely shut down the Hawkeye running attack in their Oct. 6, 2001, meeting in West Lafayette, Ind., holding Iowa to a measly 33 yards rushing on 34 carries. Only a stingy defense kept Ferentz's squad in the game, but Purdue pulled out a 23-14 victory. Naturally, revenge is on the minds of all the Hawkeyes, but the offensive line in particular is eager to prove that last year's lapse was just that.

"I think we have something to prove to ourselves," Porter said. "They came up there ready last year, and we really weren't ready. We have to prove to ourselves that it was a fluke, that it wasn't them, it was us."

On Sept. 28, Iowa shut down Penn State's defensive line, a unit with several NFL-bound players. However, as both Porter and Nelson are quick to point out, Purdue's defense style is fundamentally different from the Nittany Lions', meaning Iowa can't afford to sit back and enjoy its new national ranking.

"I don't think our coaches will let us underestimate [Purdue]," Porter said. "Practices get pretty intense, especially when we're running against a good defense like Purdue. If you step wrong, you're getting yelled at. If your head is in the wrong place, you're getting yelled at."

Nelson emphasized the Boilermakers' speed on defense, something that gave Iowa fits in 2001, but also noted that this year's Hawkeye line is prepared for anything.

"They presented some things that were tough tactically [last year]," he said. "If the defense is fast, you really have to be on your horse and drive your feet. There really isn't anything you can do; the speed you have now is the speed you'll have in the game. You just try to utilize your strengths and minimize your weaknesses."

With that in mind as they play their last Homecoming game at Kinnick, the four senior offensive lineman hope to atone for last year's slip, as well as opening up a big hole for Iowa to run through to a conference title. And that, ultimately, fulfills a plan years in the making. As Ferentz put it, "Our plan was to ride those guys, and they've done a great job of responding."

LEFT:
Hawkeye offensive linemen Andy Lightfoot, David Porter, Bruce Nelson, Ben Sobieski and Eric Steinbach jog off the Kinnick Stadium field for the final time as players following Iowa's win over Northwestern. Lucas Underwood/The Daily Iowan

ABOVE:
The Iowa offensive line readies for the snap. Ben Plank/The Daily Iowan

SATURDAY, SEPTEMBER 28, 2002
IOWA HAWKEYES 42 AT PENN STATE NITTANY LIONS 35

HAPPY VALLEY
HAPPY ENDING - AGAIN

Hawks win in OT at Penn State for the second time; drop Nittany Lions, 42-35

BY TODD BROMMELKAMP
DAILY IOWAN ASSISTANT SPORTS EDITOR

STATE COLLEGE, Pa.—They say lightning doesn't strike the same place twice, but both Penn State and Iowa felt thunderstruck when they found themselves tied at the end of regulation for the second time in as many visits to Beaver Stadium.

"It was an eerie feeling the whole second half," Iowa kicker Nate Kaeding, the hero of Iowa's 26-23 double-overtime victory here two years ago, said.

And as with Iowa's victory over the Nittany Lions in 2000, it was the defense that rescued the Hawkeyes from the clutches of defeat. Penn State had an opportunity to tie the game again in overtime, but under heavy pressure from Iowa's Jonathan Babineaux, Zack Mills's pass on fourth down and four hit center Joe Iorio in the back of the helmet and fell harmlessly to the ground as the Hawkeyes swarmed onto the field in celebration. Safety Ryan Hansen intercepted a Penn State pass on the same side of the field two years ago to secure victory for the Hawks.

The play allowed a six-yard pass from Brad Banks to C. J. Jones to be the difference in Iowa's wild 42-35 victory over No. 12 Penn State in front of 108,247 fans—the largest crowd ever to watch an Iowa football game.

"Just give it all I got, this is the last play of the game, if we stop them, it's over," the converted fullback Babineaux recalled thinking to himself while lining up for what indeed turned out to be the final down of the game. "I was just trying to get pressure on the quarterback."

Oddly enough the game was just the second overtime contest for both schools, the first being their last meeting in Happy Valley.

Iowa's victory over Penn State marked the first time the Hawkeyes defeated a ranked opponent since they stunned No. 12 Northwestern in 2000. It was the first time they had done so on the road since 1996 when they stunned Penn State, ranked No. 8 at the time.

RIGHT:

Hawkeyes kicker Nate Kaeding reacts after hitting a 55-yard field goal in the second quarter. Zach Boyden-Holmes/The Daily Iowan

ABOVE:

Hawkeyes tight end Dallas Clark makes a fingertip catch as Penn State defender Shawn Mayer closes in for the tackle. Zach Boyden-Holmes/The Daily Iowan

The topsy-turvy finish was a happy ending to what very well could have turned in to a Happy Valley nightmare for the Hawkeyes. Iowa watched helplessly as the Nittany Lions clawed away at a 35-13 lead during the fourth quarter, capitalizing on Iowa turnovers and scoring touchdowns on their final three possessions to force yet another overtime contest.

"I was pleased the kids came back the way they did and I was disappointed that we didn't play better," said Penn State coach Joe Paterno.

For the Hawkeyes it was impossible to watch the dramatic shift in momentum toward Penn State during the second half and not recall their 36-31 loss to Iowa State Sept. 14.

"We had kind of a similar situation two weeks ago and didn't answer the bell," Iowa coach Kirk Ferentz, who along with former Alabama coach Bill Curry and Michigan's Lloyd Carr becomes just the third coach ever to defeat Paterno three consecutive times. "I was hoping that we would learn from the Iowa State game."

Not unlike Iowa's meltdown against Iowa State, which saw the Hawkeyes fumble twice in the third quarter,

ABOVE:
Iowa's Jonathan Babineaux agrees with the referees' call during Iowa's victory over Penn State. Zach Boyden-Holmes/The Daily Iowan

	1st	2nd	3rd	4th	OT	FINAL
IOWA	**17**	**9**	**9**	**0**	**7**	**42**
PENN STATE	**0**	**7**	**6**	**22**	**0**	**35**

SCORING SUMMARY

QTR	TEAM	PLAY		TIME
1st	**HAWKEYES**	TD	Jones 4-yd. pass from Banks (Kaeding kick)	9:34
1st	**HAWKEYES**	FG	Kaeding 47-yd.	4:51
1st	**HAWKEYES**	TD	Russell 20-yd. run (Kaeding kick)	3:46
2nd	**HAWKEYES**	TD	Hinkel 22-yd. pass from Banks (Blocked XP)	6:04
2nd	**NITTANY LIONS**	TD	B. Johnson 28-yd. pass from Mills (Gould Kick)	1:25
2nd	**HAWKEYES**	FG	Kaeding 55-yd.	0:00
3rd	**NITTANY LIONS**	TD	L. Johnson 1-yd. run (Blocked XP)	10:32
3rd	**HAWKEYES**	ST	Johnson extra point return	10:32
3rd	**HAWKEYES**	FG	Brown 54-yd. pass from Banks (Kaeding kick)	7:03
4th	**NITTANY LIONS**	TD	L. Johnson 36-yd. pass from Mills (Gould Kick)	7:13
4th	**NITTANY LIONS**	TD	T. Johnson 44-yd. pass from Mills (Ganter 2 pt. run)	3:51
4th	**NITTANY LIONS**	TD	B.Johnson 8-yd. pass from Mills (Gould Kick)	1:20
OT	**HAWKEYES**	TD	Jones 6-yd. pass from Banks (Kaeding kick)	)0:00

———— OFFENSE ————

HAWKEYES

PASSING	ATT	COMP	YDS	INT	TD
Banks	30	18	261	2	4

RECEIVING	CATCHES	YDS	TD
Jones	7	46	2
Brown	4	100	1
Clark	4	88	0
Hinkel	2	28	1
Jackson	1	-1	0

RUSHING	RUSHES	YDS	TD
Russell	35	142	1
Banks	8	41	0
Lewis	4	18	0
Cervantes	2	8	0

NITTANY LIONS

PASSING	ATT	COMP	YDS	INT	TD
Mills	44	23	399	2	4

RECEIVING	CATCHES	YDS	TD
B. Johnson	7	146	2
L. Johnson	6	93	1
T. Johnson	4	111	1
Williams	4	48	0
McHugh	1	1	0

RUSHING	RUSHES	YDS	TD
L. Johnson	18	68	1
Robinson	4	-2	0
Mills	4	-10	0

ABOVE:

Hawkeyes linebacker Matt Roth sacks Nittany Lions quarterback Zack Mills. Zach Boyden-Holmes/The Daily Iowan

it was their own sloppy play that gave Penn State its opportunity to return to the game. After Ed Hinkel returned a Penn State punt 54 yards to the 12-yard line, quarterback Brad Banks was picked off by Bryan Scott in the end zone when tight end Dallas Clark slipped and fell to the ground. Iowa got the ball back two plays later when Jovon Johnson snared a Mills pass and returned it to the one-yard line, but running back Fred Russell fumbled at the line of scrimmage, making it two consecutive possessions in which the Hawkeyes could have soundly closed the door on Penn State.

"We did have a chance to make it a controllable ballgame," Ferentz said.

The extra breathing room was just what the Nittany Lions needed. Mills hit running back Larry Johnson with a 36-yard pass with 7:13 remaining in the game to pull the team within 15 points, 35-20. After forcing Iowa to go three and out, it took Mills just one play to hit Tony Johnson with a 44-yard scoring strike capped off by a fake extra point by Robbie Gould, which backup quarterback Chris Ganter ran in to the end zone to make

the score 35-28. Iowa had one last opportunity to run down the clock with a sustained drive, but managed to earn just one first down before punting to the Penn State 36-yard line. Mills took just five plays and one minute to connect with Bryant Johnson to tie the game at 35.

Mills threw for 399 yards on the day, the most allowed by an Iowa defense this season, on 23-of-44 passing.

Lost in the shuffle of all the scoring was a little-noticed two points put on the board in the third quarter after Iowa's D. J. Johnson returned a blocked extra point 99 yards following a Larry Johnson one-yard touchdown run. It extended Iowa's lead to 28-13 and provided a momentary setback in momentum for the Nittany Lions. It also would eventually prove to be the difference maker in the game's outcome.

"That ended up being major," said Ferentz.

Iowa's second-half performance stood in stark contrast to the way the Hawkeyes came out in the first half, essentially silencing a raucous crowd by storming to a 23-0 lead halfway through the second quarter. Banks

"IT TOOK A LITTLE WHILE FOR THE DEFENSE TO UNDER-STAND WHAT [IOWA'S] OFFENSE WAS DOING. BY THE TIME WE FIGURED IT OUT, IT WAS A LITTLE TOO LATE.

—PENN STATE LINEBACKER LAMAR STEWART

ABOVE:
Penn State's Larry Johnson leaps over the Hawkeyes' defense to score a touchdown in the third quarter. Zach Boyden-Holmes/The Daily Iowan

ABOVE:

Hawkeyes running back Fred Russell eludes Penn State defenders. Russell gained 154 yards on the ground. Zach Boyden-Holmes/The Daily Iowan

drove the Hawkeyes 80 yards on the game's opening drive, finally connecting with Jones for a four-yard score. Kaeding added a 47-yard field goal and Iowa got touchdowns from a Fred Russell 20-yard run and wide receiver Ed Hinkel's 22-yard touchdown reception before the Nittany Lions could find the scoreboard. Russell's touchdown was set up when linebacker Fred Barr forced a Penn State fumble, and Hinkel's score was helped out when Derek Pagel intercepted a Mills pass near midfield.

"It took a little while for the defense to understand what [Iowa's] offense was doing," said Penn State linebacker LaMar Stewart. "By the time we figured it out, it was a little too late."

Bryant Johnson seemingly gave the Nittany Lions momentum heading in to halftime when he caught a 28-yard pass from Mills for Penn State's first score of the game with just 1:25 remaining in the half, but Iowa marched 42 yards to the 38-yard line where Kaeding connected on a career-long 55-yard field goal—the third longest in school history.

Kaeding's streak of consecutive PATs ended at 60 when his third attempt of the day was blocked by Penn State's Derek Wake, but his two field goals broke his own school record of 11 consecutive connections, which he set last season.

Banks finished the game 18 of 30, passing for 261 yards and four touchdowns. Russell recorded his fourth 100-yard-plus rushing performance of the year with 142 yards on 35 carries. Maurice Brown was Iowa's leading receiver with four catches for an even 100 yards.

Larry Johnson was Penn State's leading rusher, carrying 18 times for 68 yards while Bryant Johnson led Nittany Lion receivers with eight catches for 146 yards.

Saturday's victory marks the first time Iowa has started the season 4-1 since 1997, and gives the Hawkeyes confidence heading in to a pair of home games with Purdue and Michigan State.

" *IT WAS AN EERIE FEELING THE WHOLE SECOND HALF.* "

— IOWA KICKER NATE KAEDING

ABOVE:
Iowa's Fred Barr lays a monster hit on Penn State running back Larry Johnson, causing a fumble. Zach Boyden-Holmes/The Daily Iowan

"
WE TURNED IT LOOSE A LITTLE BIT [AGAINST PENN STATE]. WE GOT A CHANCE TO TURN IT LOOSE ON THE PASS RUSH. "

—Iowa defensive lineman
Jared Clauss

SATURDAY, OCTOBER 5, 2002

PURDUE BOILERMAKERS 28 AT IOWA HAWKEYES 31

HAWKS HAVE A HAPPY HOMECOMING

Last minute TD, interception provide Iowa with 31-28 victory over Purdue

BY TODD BROMMELKAMP
DAILY IOWAN ASSISTANT SPORTS EDITOR

No overtime was needed, but for the second consecutive week the No. 24 Iowa Hawkeyes made sure fans got more than their money's worth with another thrilling last-minute victory.

Iowa quarterback Brad Banks provided for a happy Homecoming in Iowa City, hitting tight end Dallas Clark with a seven-yard scoring strike with just 1:07 remaining in the game, and defensive back Adolphus Shelton intercepted a Brandon Kirsch pass deep in Iowa territory with seconds remaining to preserve a wild 31-28 Hawkeye victory.

Banks finished the day with 226 yards and two touchdowns on 14-of-22 passing. He also carried five times for 51 yards.

"Brad kept his focus out there and that's what he had to do," said Iowa coach Kirk Ferentz. "If he's not in control out there it's tough."

Standeford fell into the hands of Shelton on the Iowa 17-yard line.

"Everything happened so fast," Shelton said. "The quarterback threw to my man, the defensive line got good pressure, and the receiver misjudged the throw."

Iowa improves to 5-1 and a perfect 2-0 in the Big Ten for the first time since 1996. Purdue falls to 3-3, 1-1 in the Big Ten.

Kirsch led Purdue back down the field on the final drive of the game, starting on the Boilers' own 21-yard line, but his pass to John

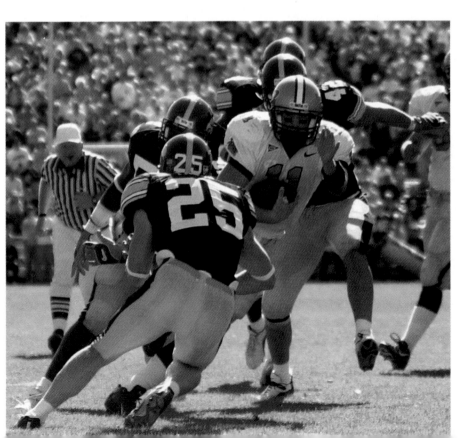

RIGHT:

Purdue quarterback Brandon Kirsch breaks through the Iowa defense. Kirsch gained 38 yards on 14 carries. Whitney Kidder/ The Daily Iowan

ABOVE:

Hawkeyes receiver Maurice Brown is brought down by Boilermaker defenders Ralph Turner and Joe Odom. Lucas Underwood/The Daily Iowan

Purdue rallied from a 24-14 deficit in the fourth quarter after a 16-yard touchdown run by Kirsch and a two-yard score by Jon Goldsberry to take a 28-24 lead with just 5:45 remaining in the game. Iowa appeared to lose its last opportunity for a comeback when Banks was sacked on fourth and long with just 2:44 remaining, but the Boilermakers quickly went three and out, setting the stage for more last-minute Iowa heroics.

"That was great to get that other chance," said Clark, who tied a career high with 116 yards on three catches—two for scores.

On the first play of Iowa's final possession, Banks ran a keeper 44 yards to the Purdue 43-yard line after beginning the drive on the Iowa 13. Banks then hit Mo Brown along the sideline for a 20-yard gain, and after an incomplete pass hooked up with Clark for a 14-yard gainer down to the Purdue nine for a shot at the game-winning score.

Clark's only other catch of the day was a 95-yard connection with Banks from Iowa's own five-yard line. Clark tiptoed over a Purdue defender and raced down the left sideline before reaching the end zone to tie the

BELOW:
Hawkeyes defensive back Antwan Allen brings down Purdue kick returner Anthony Chambers. Whitney Kidder/The Daily Iowan

	1st	2nd	3rd	4th	Final
PURDUE	7	7	0	14	28
IOWA	3	7	14	7	31

SCORING SUMMARY

QTR	TEAM	PLAY		TIME
1st	**HAWKEYES**	FG	Kaeding 51-yd.	3:49
1st	**BOILERMAKERS**	TD	Standeford 61-yd. pass from Orton (Lacevic kick)	1:16
2nd	**BOILERMAKERS**	TD	Void 1-yd. run (Lacevic kick)	11:15
2nd	**HAWKEYES**	TD	Allen 85-yd. blocked FG return (Kaeding kick)	1:20
3rd	**HAWKEYES**	TD	Roberts 0-yd. blocked punt return (Kaeding kick)	12:48
3rd	**HAWKEYES**	TD	Clark 95-yd. pass from Banks (Kaeding kick)	2:37
4th	**BOILERMAKERS**	TD	Kirsch 16-yd. run (Lacevic kick)	10:23
4th	**BOILERMAKERS**	TD	Goldsberry 2-yd. run (Lacevic kick)	5:45
4th	**HAWKEYES**	TD	Clark 7-yd. pass from Banks (Kaeding kick)	1:07

———— OFFENSE ————

BOILERMAKERS

PASSING	ATT	COMP	YDS	INT	TD
Orton	37	22	247	0	1
Kirsch	21	13	163	1	0
Rhinehart	1	0	0	1	0

RECEIVING	CATCHES	YDS	TD
Stubblefield	13	149	0
Standeford	6	105	1
James	5	38	0
Morales	5	30	0
Rhinehart	4	68	0
Rucks	1	14	0
Harris	1	6	0

RUSHING	RUSHES	YDS	TD
Kirsch	6	49	1
Harris	14	35	0
Orton	6	8	0
Void	2	3	1
Goldsberry	1	2	1

HAWKEYES

PASSING	ATT	COMP	YDS	INT	TD
Banks	22	14	226	0	2

RECEIVING	CATCHES	YDS	TD
Hinkel	4	30	0
Clark	3	116	2
Brown	3	47	0
Jones	3	27	0
Solomon	1	6	0

RUSHING	RUSHES	YDS	TD
Russell	22	109	0
Banks	5	30	0
Greving	5	15	0
Cervantes	3	4	0

BRAD [BANKS] KEPT HIS FO-CUS OUT THERE AND THAT'S WHAT HE HAD TO DO. IF HE'S NOT IN CONTROL OUT THERE ITS TOUGH.

—IOWA HEAD COACH
KIRK FERENTZ

LEFT:
Iowa tight end Dallas Clark hauls in the game-winning touchdown pass from Brad Banks with one minute left in the fourth quarter.
Lucas Underwood/The Daily
Iowan

ABOVE:
Iowa running back Fred Russell breaks through the Purdue defense. Russell gained 121 yards on 22 carries.
Whitney Kidder/The Daily Iowan

record for longest pass play in school history. Chuck Hartlieb connected with Quinn Early for a 95-yard gain against Northwestern in 1987.

"I think I'm still tyring to catch my breath," he joked after the game.

The more appropriate question would be to ask what could be said for Iowa's special teams, which accounted for 17 points Saturday. Nate Kaeding provided the Hawks with a 3-0 lead on a 51-yard field goal, and Iowa scored a pair of special teams touchdowns when Antwan Allen returned a blocked field goal by Bob Sanders 85 yards in the second quarter and Jermire Roberts fell on a blocked punt by Sean Considine in the end zone early in the third quarter.

"Special teams play helped out big-time today," said Banks.

The effort on special teams turned out to be a difference maker as the Boilermakers rolled over Iowa's defense for 507 yards of total offense, including 410 through the air. Purdue held an early 14-3 lead prior to the touchdowns by Allen and Roberts. Quarterback Kyle

Orton hit John Standeford for a 61-yard touchdown near the end of the first quarter and Jerod Void pounded the ball in from the one-yard line on Purdue's first possession of the second quarter.

Orton, a native of Altoona, Iowa, threw for 247 yards and one touchdown, completing 22 of 37 passes before being removed from the game near the end of the third quarter. Purdue coach Joe Tiller said following the game that Orton could not recall the last play he ran on the field after being hit hard by an Iowa player. Kirsch threw for 163 yards and completed 13 of 21 passes, including the interception that ended the game.

"I thought he deserved better than that, to have the ball go off the hands of our own player to them," Tiller said of Shelton's interception.

Iowa's Fred Russell posted his fifth 100-yard rushing day of the year, leading the Hawkeyes with 109 yards on 22 attempts. Kirsch was the Boilermakers' leading rusher, accumulating 49 of Purdue's 97 yards on the ground—the most allowed by Iowa this season.

ABOVE:
Hawkeyes defensive back Antwan Allen breaks up
a Boilermaker play. Allen finished with five tackles.
Whitney Kidder/The Daily Iowan

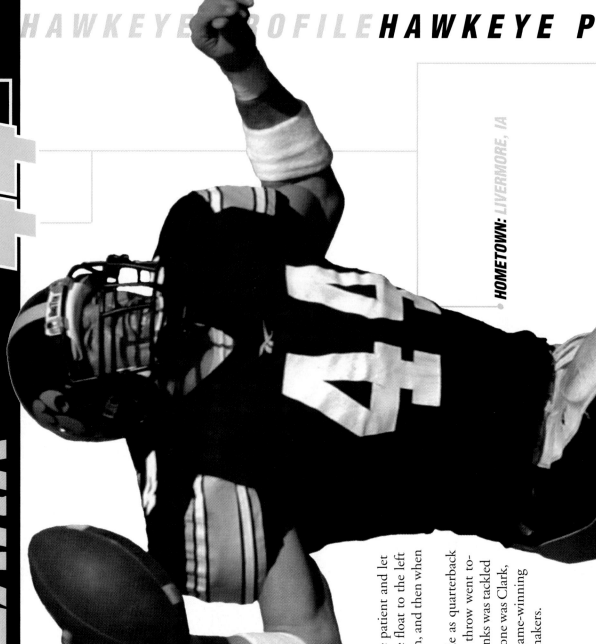

BY BRIAN TRIPLETT, DAILY IOWAN REPORTER

DALLAS CLARK

44

HOMETOWN: *LIVERMORE, IA*

In high school, Dallas Clark the quarterback knew about throwing touchdown passes. In his early days as a walk-on at Iowa, Dallas Clark the linebacker knew about trying to prevent touchdown passes.

But it wasn't until recently that Dallas Clark the tight end knew about catching passes, such as the one last week for the Hawkeyes' most crucial touchdown of the year.

A packed crowd at Kinnick Stadium waited in anticipation to see the play that would make or break the game for Iowa against Purdue. It was fourth and goal from the seven-yard line with a minute and seven seconds to play, and Clark knew his task.

"That's a type of play [where] you just need to be patient and let everything kind of unfold," he said. "Let their defense float to the left and just kind of sneak out. I think I waited long enough, and then when it gets to that point, you just gotta catch the ball."

The play seemed to be headed toward the left side as quarterback Brad Banks rolled out in that direction, but then the throw went towards the right side of the end zone moments before Banks was tackled by the Purdue defense. Waiting on that side of the end zone was Clark, who let the ball sink into his hands for the Hawkeyes' game-winning touchdown catch in the 31-28 victory over the Boilermakers.

Zach Boyden-Holmes/The Daily Iowan

AGE: 23

CLASS: JR.

TIGHT END

"That couldn't have been any more beautiful," Iowa coach Kirk Ferentz said. "It's either there, or it's not. We have a couple of dummy guys out there, and hopefully, Brad doesn't go to the dummies."

That play wasn't nearly the beginning of Clark's contribution to the victory. Late in the third quarter, when Iowa was on its own five-yard line on third and seven, Clark caught a short pass from Banks, broke a tackle, and sprinted 95 yards down the field for a touchdown. The play, which gave the Hawkeyes a 24-14 edge, tied for the longest pass play in Iowa football history.

"They had pretty much their whole defense within 10 yards of the line of scrimmage, and so all we had to do was get something over that," Clark said. "I was able to get to the sideline and just had to make one guy miss. I'm definitely not the fastest guy out there, it's just that I had the right angle and the opportunity."

Opportunity was not something that Clark, who was named to the *Football News* preseason All-America third team, saw a lot of early this season. It was not until the Hawkeyes' fourth game against Utah State that Clark caught his first pass of the year. The lack of immediate success did not seem to put much of a damper on things for him, however.

"Whether I get the ball or not, that doesn't matter, just as long as Brad makes the right decision to get us the first downs and the touchdowns," he said.

In the nail-biting win over Purdue on Oct. 5, Clark proved to be more than just an offensive contributor. He matched a career-high 116 yards on three receptions, including Iowa's only two offensive touchdowns, and his late-game heroics helped earn him Big Ten Offensive Player of the Week honors.

It seems incredible that it wasn't until a year and a half ago that Clark knew anything about the role of tight end. The Livermore, Iowa, native attended Twin River Valley High School, where he played both quarterback and linebacker. He came to Iowa in 1998 but was only a part-time student because of a broken collarbone, so his football eligibility did not begin until the 1999 season. Clark walked on to the football team but decided to redshirt because of surgery on his collarbone and appendix.

As a redshirt freshman, Clark saw time at linebacker and on special teams, but it wasn't until the spring of his sophomore year that he began playing tight end. Clark learned the role quickly, gaining 539 yards and four touchdowns in his sophomore campaign.

"Now that I look at it, it's definitely more rewarding catching a big touchdown than making a big tackle," he said. Whether he's throwing a touchdown, stopping a touchdown, or catching one, it seems as if Dallas Clark was born to play football. It just took some time for him to find his place.

81

Photo courtesy of Curtis Lehmkuhl/The Daily Iowan

Photo courtesy of Lucas Underwood/The Daily Iowan

FRIDAY, OCTOBER 4, 2002

Riding the roller coaster

Iowa native Pagel now seeing benefits from tough decisions

BY ROSEANNA SMITH
DAILY IOWAN SPORTS EDITOR

Jeanette Pagel can't talk about dark days in the spring of 2000 without choking up and fighting back tears. She doesn't want to remember the phone call when her son, Derek, free safety on the Iowa secondary, almost walked away from the team with a broken heart.

She does remember Derek's tears, though, after the spring game when he walked out of the locker room distraught. She watched as the roller coaster of her son's Iowa career began.

After walking on to the Hawkeye squad with a single chance to make it and a dump-truck load of hope, Pagel spent a redshirt season on the bench, watching and learning.

"I was a recruited walk-on, but I never had an official visit," Pagel said. "I honestly think I was recruited here to be a scout-team football player. They bring good athletes in, and those guys are important to good football teams, but I don't think they were very concerned whether I came to Iowa or not."

A decorated player from Plainfield, Iowa, Pagel won first-team All-State honors as a running back in his senior year and as a punter in his junior year. He was voted most valuable back in the district, rushing 184 times for 1,163 yards and scoring 17 touchdowns. He didn't just play football, accumulating letters in baseball, basketball, and track as well.

Derek wrestled with the idea of even joining the Iowa team—taking a risk walking on with no scholarship and no guarantees—or going to Wartburg, where he could play every down as a hero.

But the choice seemed to narrow as he looked around the basement of his parents' house—decorated wall to wall in black and gold. There were the memories of cookouts and parties hosted in the garage, where the television was always tuned to Iowa football, the hamburgers were always sizzling on the grill, and the fans flocked sometimes in groups of 100 to see how the Hawkeyes fared each weekend. He remembered a picture taken with Hayden Fry.

ABOVE:
Derek Pagel sheds a tear after his final home game at Kinnick Stadium against Northwestern. John Richard/The Daily Iowan

"Our house isn't painted in black and gold, but it's close," Derek's father, Richard Pagel, said. "It was a tough time for the family and for him. I always wanted him to attend the UI; I've been a fan since 1962, when I was in high school, but it wasn't an easy thing to do to tell someone to excel in something that hard to do."

Derek looked at his letters, awards, and himself, and took one giant leap of faith.

He would be disappointed.

He received limited playing time in all 11 games in 1999 on special teams, but after being looked over for reps in the 2000 spring game, he made the call home.

"At that point, I was ready to leave," Pagel said. "I was just as down as anyone could be in a football career. I didn't even know if I wanted to play football or just go to school, become a student, or transfer and go somewhere where I knew I could play.

"I was just so down. I said I'll stick it out one more summer here, work out, and go through camp. I knew even if I went through camp and I didn't like what was going on, I'd still have time to transfer to another school."

Heavily recruited out of high school by Wartburg, where his older brother Dallas was a senior, Derek considered his options and made arrangements to reevaluate the situation after fall camp in 2000. He had all but packed his bags before he talked first to his brother, then to Iowa football coach Kirk Ferentz and assistant Bret Bielema.

"We have a different brother relationship—he's my best friend," Dallas Pagel said. "Every day I'd talk to him on the phone at least once or twice. I told him, 'You've made it this far; if you want to leave and play football at Wartburg, that's what you need to do.'

"He's an athlete, and it's hard for a competitor to sit on the sidelines. It was a really tough decision for him, but I think that's why he went to the coaches."

A positive meeting, position change, and 10 pounds later, Derek was on his way. He began working on third-down situations and played in 10 of 12 games that fall, recording 11 solo tackles, six assists, one sack, and three pass deflections.

The roller coaster was beginning to head uphill.

In 2001, Pagel started in six of the 12 games he played, recording season totals of 28 solo tackles, 16 assists, three tackles for loss, one recovered fumble, one interception, and four pass break-ups. He was chosen as a team captain against Michigan and Texas Tech, and he felt like he was gaining ground—literally.

The roller coaster chugged along on Dec. 29, 2001, when he played a role in Iowa's 19-16 win against Texas Tech at the Alamo Bowl. Though he posted humble numbers of two solo tackles, two assists, and one pass break-up, Pagel proved his worth on the gridiron and off.

He met his parents, who travel to every home and away game sporting Derek's No. 25 jersey, at the hotel after the victory and changed into street clothes for dinner.

"He didn't want to be decorated like a superjock hero," Richard said.

"He was on the winning team, but he didn't want to go downtown and have everyone around—he's just like that—he doesn't want to take all that credit."

On the field, Pagel proved his mettle during the spring game, recording five tackles including one for a loss, after which he finally saw his name—under the first-team free-safety slot.

"The coaches gave him their confidence," Dallas said.

"He went in knowing he was the starting free safety, and it was his job to lose. He didn't have to worry about it any more."

Though Derek's day in the limelight has finally arrived, he hasn't quit working. He recorded eight tackles against Iowa State and had a career day in Iowa's 42-35 overtime win at Penn State on Sept. 28. Pagel came up with his second interception of the season and the third of his career in the second quarter. He also blocked a PAT attempt that was returned 99 yards by defensive back D. J. Johnson. He finished the game with eight total tackles and an excitement he'd never felt before.

"It's an amazing feeling," Pagel said. "It's been so up and down. The highs are so high, and the lows are so low it's just incredible. Really in my career right now, I think I'm running on high."

Sitting in the 12th row, three seats in, Dallas Pagel switched seats with his dad between third and fourth down at the end of the Penn State's overtime possession before rushing down to the front row as quarterback Zack Mills failed to convert a screen pass on the five-yard line.

"I darted down to the front—it was crazy," Dallas said. "Just to be there, to celebrate that moment with him was a highlight in my life. It was probably his biggest game so far."

And members of Derek's family haven't been the only ones noticing his progress and success. Ferentz said he was pleased with Pagel's efforts and anticipated more good things from the senior.

"He wanted to give it up three years ago, but he stuck it out, and the rest is history," Ferentz said.

"I wouldn't say I talked him into it; we [the football staff] counseled him a little bit and encouraged him, but it was his decision to make.

"I think he's got a chance to play a lot more football after this year. It's a story that's going to turn out really well, I think."

Though Derek said he was focusing on graduating in December with a finance degree instead of thinking about a future in the NFL, the door is still wide open.

His father says it always has been.

"He knows what it's like to taste defeat—to be stepped on and to come back up. He wants to go to Pasadena to the Rose Bowl, and I think he'll do it, too."

BELOW:
Iowa defensive back Derek Pagel intercepts a pass intended for Wisconsin receiver Jonathon Orr as teammate Bob Sanders looks on. Zach Boyden-Holmes/The Daily Iowan

SATURDAY, OCTOBER 12, 2002

MICHIGAN STATE 16 AT IOWA HAWKEYES 44

HAWKEYES HUMBLE SPARTANS IN 44-16 ROUT

Iowa scores 44 straight points; improves to 6-1

BY TODD BROMMELKAMP
DAILY IOWAN ASSISTANT SPORTS EDITOR

Michigan State scored first and Michigan State scored last. But in between it was all Iowa Saturday afternoon inside Kinnick Stadium.

The Hawkeyes scored 44 unanswered points before a late Spartan score en route to an impressive 44-16 victory over Michigan State in Iowa City. Iowa, ranked No. 17 in the country heading in to the game, improved to 6-1 for the first time since 1991. The Hawkeyes are a perfect 3-0 in Big Ten play.

After weeks of fine-tuning and struggling to put four quarters of solid football together, Iowa had no problem doing just that Saturday as it dominated Michigan State from start to finish.

"A lot of people have been doubting us after the last two wins against Penn State and Purdue, but I think this added a lot of validity to our season," said Iowa kicker Nate Kaeding.

Kaeding moved in to third place on the school's all-time scoring list with 221 career points. The junior was a perfect three of three on field goal attempts from 28, 36, and 43 yards to extend his streak of consecutive field goals made to 17.

Iowa capitalized on five Michigan State turnovers in the game, including three interceptions, two of which came in the first quarter of play, to account for 20 of its points.

"It is very, very hard to play over the number of turnovers we had," said Michigan State coach Bobby Williams, whose team falls to 3-3 this season and 1-1 in Big Ten play.

With the game knotted at seven in the first quarter, Iowa's Bob Sanders pulled in a Jeff Smoker pass along the

RIGHT:

Hawkeyes wide receiver Maurice Brown tries to prevent an interception by Spartans cornerback Cedric Henry. Curtis Lehmkuhl/ The Daily Iowan

ABOVE:
Hawkeyes wide receiver C. J. Jones scores on a 62-yard reception in the second quarter. Stephanie McNiel/The Daily Iowan

sidelines which eventually led to Kaeding's 36-yard field goal. On Michigan State's next possession, Derek Pagel intercepted a Smoker offering and returned it 62 yards for a score to put Iowa up 17-7.

"The first half was all big plays," Iowa coach Kirk Ferentz said.

After allowing an opening scoring drive of 54 yards, which was capped by Dawan Moss's two-yard touchdown run, Iowa's Jermelle Lewis returned the kick 94 yards to even the score. That seemed to set the tempo for the ensuing three quarters of play.

Iowa capped the first half with a 62-yard touchdown pass from Brad Banks to C. J. Jones and a 43-yarder by Kaeding.

The Iowa defense did its part as well, holding the Spartans to just 249 yards of total offense, including just 55 on the ground. All-American wideout Charles Rogers finished the game with a team-high 78 yards receiving,

but failed to add to his NCAA record of touchdown receptions in a game. After beginning against Iowa last October, the streak numbered 13 games before Saturday.

"Give credit to both their safeties," Rogers said in a statement following the game. "They did a great job not only of stopping the run, but also a good job in pass support."

The 194 yards passing by the Spartans was a season low for an Iowa opponent. Smoker finished the day 17 of 33 for 169 yards, one touchdown and two interceptions. Backup Damon Dowdell didn't fare any better, completing just five attempts for 25 yards and throwing one interception. Much of Michigan State's inability to pick apart Iowa's defense had to do with the heavy heat both quarterbacks felt from the defensive line.

"They didn't dominate us from a physical standpoint," Williams said. "We turned the ball over too many times; we had a lot of passes overthrown."

BELOW:
Hawkeyes running back Aaron Greving attempts to rush past the Spartans in the second quarter.
Stephanie McNiel/The Daily Iowan

	1st	2nd	3rd	4th	Final
MICHIGAN STATE	7	0	0	9	16
IOWA	17	10	17	0	44

SCORING SUMMARY

QTR	TEAM	PLAY		TIME
1st	**SPARTANS**	TD	Moss 2-yd. run (Rayner kick)	7:38
1st	**HAWKEYES**	TD	Lewis 94-yd. kick return (Kaeding kick)	7:21
1st	**HAWKEYES**	FG	Kaeding 36-yd.	2:35
1st	**HAWKEYES**	TD	Pagel 62-yd. interception return (Kaeding kick)	0:25
2nd	**HAWKEYES**	TD	Jones 62-yd. pass from Banks (Kaeding kick)	6:22
2nd	**HAWKEYES**	FG	Kaeding 43-yd.	0:25
3rd	**HAWKEYES**	TD	Russell 9-yd. run (Kaeding kick)	11:54
3rd	**HAWKEYES**	FG	Kaeding 28-yd.	8:50
3rd	**HAWKEYES**	TD	Jones 25-yd. pass from Banks (Kaeding kick)	1:32
4th	**SPARTANS**	TD	Lovett 20-yd. pass from Smoker (Rayner kick)	7:59
4th	**SPARTANS**	ST	Team safety	2:11

OFFENSE

SPARTANS

PASSING	ATT	COMP	YDS	INT	TD
Smoker	33	17	169	2	1
Dowdell	13	5	25	1	0

RECEIVING	CATCHES	YDS	TD
Lovett	7	68	1
Rogers	5	78	0
Richard	4	5	0
Shabaj	2	18	0
Kavanaght	2	14	0
Goebel	1	7	0
Woods	1	4	0

RUSHING	RUSHES	YDS	TD
Moss	16	24	1
Richard	6	23	0
Smoker	7	8	0
Dowdell	3	0	0
Hayes	1	0	0

HAWKEYES

PASSING	ATT	COMP	YDS	INT	TD
Banks	19	8	154	1	2
Chandler	2	1	3	0	0

RECEIVING	CATCHES	YDS	TD
Jones	2	87	2
Clark	2	30	0
Brown	2	20	0
Solomon	2	9	0
Jackson	1	11	0

RUSHING	RUSHES	YDS	TD
Russell	18	75	1
Banks	9	36	0
Greving	7	13	0
Lewis	2	4	0
Chandler	1	3	0
Mickens	1	0	0

Iowa recorded four sacks, three by sophomore defensive end Matt Roth, and 11 tackles for a loss.

"I was very pleased to see how hard the defensive line played today," Ferentz said. "They were able to force some holding calls and put pressure on Michigan State."

"I think late in the third quarter when [Smoker] kept getting knocked down and getting up slower and slower we knew we had the game," said defensive tackle Colin Cole.

If Smoker's effort slowed in the second half, Iowa's only picked up steam.

"That was a big emphasis for us that we didn't want to come out in the second half and let down like we had," defensive tackle Jared Clauss said. "And we definitely didn't let down in the second half."

Running back Fred Russell reached the end zone for a nine-yard score on the Hawkeyes' first possession of the second half to extend the team's lead to 34-7. Russell finished the day with a team-leading 75 yards rushing.

BELOW:
Hawkeyes linebacker Matt Roth tackles Spartans quarterback Damon Dowdell, causing a fumble.
Curtis Lehmkuhl/The Daily Iowan

ABOVE:
Iowa cornerback D. J. Johnson intercepts a pass thrown by Michigan State quarterback Jeff Smoker. Curtis Lehmkuhl/The Daily Iowan

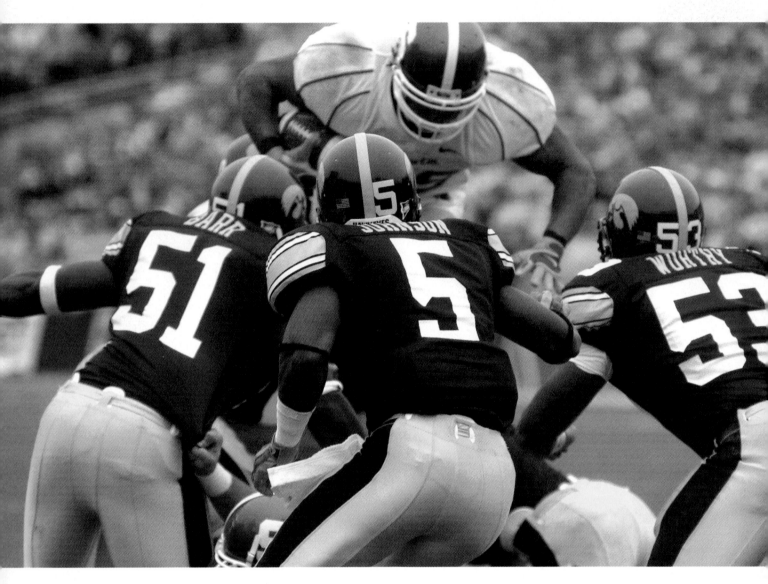

ABOVE:
Spartans tailback Dawan Moss attempts to jump over Iowa defenders and into the end zone.
Curtis Lehmkuhl/The Daily Iowan

Kaeding added his final field goal in the third as well before Banks found Jones again for a score, this time an acrobatic 25-yard reception in the back of the end zone. Jones finished the day with 87 yards receiving on just two catches.

"When it's man-on-man [coverage] like today, you're just lickin' your chops," Jones said.

Michigan State ended its scoring drought with 7:59 remaining in the fourth quarter when Smoker connected with B. J. Lovett for a 20-yard touchdown pass. The Spartans added a safety with just over two minutes remaining in the game when Iowa punter David Bradley ran roughly 15 seconds off the clock before stepping out of the end zone. The move essentially traded two points for better field position and the Spartans could not capitalize, going three and out on their final possession.

Iowa now faces back-to-back road tests against Indiana and Michigan. Ferentz said the team will not prepare any differently for those contests than it has for ones at home.

"Playing on the road can be a negative if you let it be, but it can also be a positive," he said.

ABOVE:
Hawkeyes quarterback Brad Banks gets caught in traffic. Banks gained 45 yards on nine carries. Curtis Lehmkuhl/The Daily Iowan

> *IT JUST DIDN'T SEEM LIKE WE HAD THE ZIP OR ENERGY WE PLAYED WITH IN MOST GAMES. I DON'T KNOW IF I COULD DESCRIBE IT.*

—Iowa head coach Kirk Ferentz

IOWA HAWKEYES 24 AT INDIANA HOOSIERS 8

HAWKS GIVE HOOSIERS A NOT-SO-HAPPY HOMECOMING

Iowa escapes Indiana with 24-8 victory; looks to Michigan

BY TODD BROMMELKAMP
DAILY IOWAN ASSISTANT SPORTS EDITOR

BLOOMINGTON, Ind.—In the words of Iowa tight end Dallas Clark, the Indiana Hoosiers "out-hustled, out-played, and out-hit" the Hawkeyes Saturday. But there was another important "out" Clark made sure to include in his postgame remarks.

"We're just thankful we got out with a win," he said after Iowa spoiled Indiana's Homecoming and snapped the Hoosiers' six-game home win streak with a 24-8 victory.

And make no mistake about it, the Hawkeyes are beating a path out of Bloomington and not looking back over their shoulders.

"We gave up way too many yards and we didn't play the crisp football you need to play to win consistently," Iowa coach Kirk Ferentz said.

Indiana posted 481 yards of total offense, including 186 rushing yards against an Iowa defense which entered the contest ranked No. 2 in the nation at stopping the run. Running back Brian Lewis became the first back to rush for over 100 yards against the Hawkeyes since Wisconsin's Anthony Davis gained 142 on Nov. 3, 2001. Lewis finished the day with 121 yards.

The Hoosiers also posted 335 passing yards from quarterback Gibran Hamdan, including 198 that belonged to sophomore wide receiver Courtney Roby.

But the Hawkeyes escaped victorious, remaining perfect in Big Ten play with a 4-0 mark and improving their overall record to 7-1.

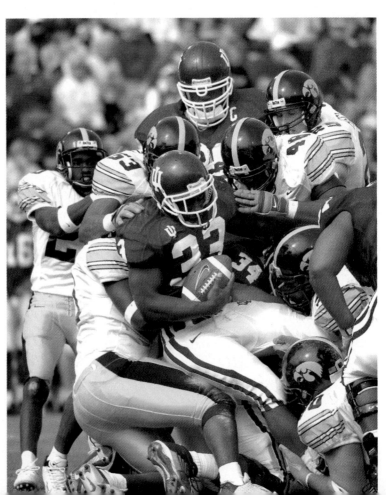

RIGHT:

The Hawkeye defense creates a wall that Hoosier running back Yamar Washington cannot break through. Lucas Underwood/ The Daily Iowan

ABOVE:
Hawkeyes linebacker Howard Hodges applies pressure to Hoosier quarterback Gibran Hamdan. Lucas Underwood/The Daily Iowan

"It was like a nightmare you couldn't wake up from, especially on my part," Roby said. "I just don't think I got it done today."

Iowa looked as if it was certainly prepared to get things done from the opening kickoff, dominating the game in the first quarter by scoring on its first three possessions and holding Indiana to three-and-out drives on the Hoosiers' first two possessions to take an early 17-0 lead.

Fred Russell scored from three yards out on Iowa's opening 80-yard drive down the field and again from two yards out after a Nate Kaeding 43-yard field goal. Russell finished the day with exactly 100 yards rushing on 19 attempts, the sixth time he has eclipsed the century mark this season.

But somewhere after Iowa's outburst it seemed as if things changed.

"We just lost focus," Russell said. "After that it seemed like we relaxed."

The Hawkeyes struggled to put together a drive, and even when they did it eventually stalled due to a penalty or intense pressure from Indiana's defense.

"Basically the story of the game was we got off to a great start then started making some mental errors," Ferentz said.

The Hawkeyes threw one interception, fumbled twice, and were flagged five times for 50 yards. However, those mental errors were countered by lapses on Indiana's

BELOW:

Iowa linebackers Fred Barr, bottom, and Kevin Worthy slam Indiana running back Yamar Washington to the ground. Lucas Underwood/The Daily Iowan

	1st	2nd	3rd	4th	Final
IOWA	**17**	**0**	**0**	**7**	**24**
INDIANA	**0**	**0**	**3**	**5**	**8**

SCORING SUMMARY

QTR	TEAM	PLAY		TIME
1st	**HAWKEYES**	TD	Russell 3-yd. run (Kaeding kick)	9:15
1st	**HAWKEYES**	FG	Kaeding 43-yd.	5:51
1sr	**HAWKEYES**	TD	Russell 2-yd. run (Kaeding kick)	4:09
3rd	**HOOSIERS**	FG	Robertson 45-yd.	8:39
4th	**HOOSIERS**	FG	Robertson 23-yd.	13:43
4th	**HAWKEYES**	TD	Brown 65-yd. pass from Banks (Kaeding kick)	11:49
4th	**HOOSIERS**	ST	Team safety	2:53

———— OFFENSE ————

HAWKEYES

PASSING	ATT	COMP	YDS	INT	TD
Banks	16	11	191	1	1

RECEIVING	CATCHES	YDS	TD
Brown	2	84	1
Clark	5	83	0
Jones	2	14	0
Cervantes	1	5	0
Hinkel	1	5	0

RUSHING	RUSHES	YDS	TD
Russell	20	110	2
Lewis	5	42	0
Greving	6	12	0
Jones	1	5	0
Banks	4	2	0

HOOSIERS

PASSING	ATT	COMP	YDS	INT	TD
Hamdan	48	21	334	3	0

RECEIVING	CATCHES	YDS	TD
Roby	11	198	0
Johnson	5	78	0
Halterman	1	24	0
Anthony	1	14	0
Spencer	1	9	0
Washington	1	6	0
Pannozzo	1	5	0

RUSHING	RUSHES	YDS	TD
Lewis	25	121	0
Washington	6	20	0
Hemdan	14	5	0

ABOVE:

Hawkeyes receiver C. J. Jones catches a pass near the goal line during a first-half drive that would lead to a touchdown.
Lucas Underwood/The Daily Iowan

part as well. After recovering a fumble by Iowa's Aaron Greving, the Hoosiers appeared to be on the brink of scoring before Iowa linebacker Grant Steen intercepted a Hamdan pass in the end zone. It was the first of three Steen interceptions for the day, all of which came in the red zone. The three picks by the former walk-on established a new school record.

"He came up with the big play time and time and time again," Ferentz said.

The junior from Emmetsburg was humbled after learning his name would be in Iowa's record books following his performance.

"They were gifts," he said. "It was the right place at the right time or whatever you call it."

ABOVE:

*Hawkeyes running back Fred Russell collides in the hole with Hoosiers
linebacker Herana-Daze Jones.* Lucas Underwood/The Daily Iowan

101

ABOVE:

Dallas Clark makes an acrobatic catch that would give the Hawkeyes a first down. Iowa went on to score on the drive. Lucas Underwood/The Daily Iowan

Had Steen not picked off Hamdan so often and in such a crucial area of the field, Indiana might have been able to repeat its upset performance over then-No. 23 Wisconsin a week before. Instead, all the Hoosiers could manage to do was put a pair of Bryan Robertson field goals from 45 and 23 yards out on the scoreboard.

"There were some critical mistakes that I made in the red zone that definitely hurt us," Hamdan said.

Hamdan, the Big Ten's Offensive Player of the Week this past week, finished the day 21 of 48 for 335 yards. His counterpart, Iowa's Brad Banks, turned in an efficient 11-of-16 day with 190 yards passing and one touchdown, a back-breaking 65-yard bomb to Mo Brown that momentarily broke Iowa out of its second-half funk early in the fourth quarter.

Iowa's victory now paves the way for a first-place showdown with undefeated Michigan next weekend in Ann Arbor. Ferentz quelled any mention of the Wolverines during this past week, but after Saturday's game he finally commented on next weekend's game.

"It's always a big game, but it's a little bigger now that we're unblemished in the conference," he said.

ABOVE:
Grant Steen throws up three fingers in reference to his third interception. All three were caught deep in Iowa territory. Lucas Underwood/The Daily Iowan

Curtis Lehmkuhl/The Daily I

DAVID PORTER

73

David Porter is not the typical college football player.

The 6'7", 320-pound fifth-year senior has been a large contributor to the success of the 9-1 Hawkeyes and their offensive line, but it is off the field where Porter's story gets interesting.

Not only is he a premed student who plays five musical instruments, but the 22-year-old has a wedding ring on his finger as well.

Porter was born in Frankfurt, Germany, where both of his parents were stationed in the military. Growing up, he grew accustomed to moving, spending his junior high days in California before moving to Illinois prior to high school.

As a fifth grader, he began playing trumpet and developed a passion for music. Along the way he also learned to play the trombone, French horn, saxophone, and tuba.

In his freshman year in high school at Althoff Catholic in Belleville, Ill., Porter decided he wanted to go into medicine.

"A lot of my family is in the medical field," he said. "I got a pretty good taste of it early on."

After graduating from high school, where he was first team All-State in football his junior and senior seasons, Porter came to Iowa, where he met Tara Fumerton in the spring of 1999. Nearly three years later, on Jan. 5, the two were married.

"I think they're a perfect couple," said Tara's father, Richard Fumerton, who is a UI professor. "He's just like a son to me."

Tara, who is older than David, will graduate along with her husband in December. The two actually share the last name Fumerton Porter, but David uses Porter for football, and Tara uses Fumerton for law.

If it weren't for Tara and her law background, Porter might be watching this year's Hawkeyes from off the field.

As a true senior last season, it seemed the team would lose Porter to graduation. But after reading through the NCAA rules and regulations,

CLASS: SR.

AGE: 22

HOMETOWN: BELLEVILLE, IL

OFFENSIVE TACKLE

Tara, who was enrolled in a law school class called Legal Issues in Intercollegiate Athletics at the time, became convinced that Porter could earn another year of eligibility by taking a medical redshirt his sophomore season.

She took her case to the coaches, who put in the petition, and Porter eventually was granted the extra year.

"I'm not sure it would have happened if it weren't for her," Tara's father said.

Her father, along with his wife, Patti, says he liked David right from the start.

"I've always thought of him as a terrific guy," Richard said.

On top of that, they've also become big fans of their son-in-law and the Hawkeyes on the field.

"My wife didn't know much about football, but she is the biggest football fan in Iowa City right now," Richard said.

Both Fumertons have made it to every one of Iowa's home games this season.

"I wear his jersey to every game, and so does my husband," Patti said. "I'm really proud that he's my son-in-law."

Tara has attended every one of Porter's games this season, home and away.

She does not go easy on her husband, however, often finding room for improvement.

"She critiques me," Porter said. "She says, 'You're not aggressive enough. You should've finished on that play. What were you doing?'

"I told the coaches, you guys are nothing compared with my wife."

On the other hand, Porter does not always let his wife get the best of him.

"I think he values my opinions on football," Tara said. "But he has no problem telling me I have no idea what I'm talking about."

Although Porter does have more responsibility than the average college athlete and is very mature for his age, he still finds time to spend with his teammates.

"We all hang out together," Porter said. "We know when it's time to be serious, but most of the time, it's not time to be serious."

Offensive linemen Will Lack and Andy Lightfoot are also premed majors.

"It's going to be a long road," Porter said, referring to medical school.

"But I think it's going to be worth it."

Along with his hopes of a future in the medical field, Porter hopes for a possible NFL career.

Don't forget that this musically talented, premed major husband—not to mention adorable around children, according to his wife—is gifted in football as well.

105

RIGHT:

Iowa's Mike Follett recovers a blocked punt in the third quarter of the Hawkeyes' win over Utah State. Curtis Lehmkuhl/The Daily Iowan

FRIDAY, OCTOBER 11, 2002

Special Recognition

Iowa's most overlooked group keeps Hawkeyes together

BY DONOVAN BURBA
DAILY IOWAN REPORTER

Here's the scene: Purdue, already up 14-3 and on the Iowa five, stalls and has to kick a field goal. Out comes the placekicker to make the short kick, usually a mere formality from that distance. Out of nowhere comes Iowa defensive back Bob Sanders, who blocks the kick. Teammate Antwan Allen recovers and runs 85 yards the other way for a touchdown. 14-10 Purdue. Halftime.

Two minutes into the third quarter, Purdue is faced with a similar circumstance. Instead of trying a field goal, the Boilermakers must punt the ball, but again, the biggest worry on a punt is the return. That is, until Sean Considine breaks through the line, blocks the punt, and it's recovered in the end zone for another Iowa touchdown. 17-14 Iowa.

Special teams aren't normally flashy; the stereotype is that special teams squads are made up of walk-ons, castoffs, has-beens, and never-will-bes. As with journalists, most of their recognition comes when they screw up. Fans equate punts, field goals, and kickoffs with commercial breaks. The kicker's on the field? Time to go to the bathroom.

But as Iowa's 31-28 win over Purdue illustrated, special teams can turn the tide of a game, or even a season. The New England Patriots won the 2002 Super Bowl behind a strong defense and underrated offense, but it was Adam Vinatieri's last-second field goal that sealed the St. Louis Rams' coffin. Weeks from now, Iowa may still be in the conference title hunt, and people will point to the Brad Banks-led game-winning drive as the defining moment of the Purdue game. But if the Hawkeyes really do win the Big Ten, or at least come close, it will be due in no small part to the special teams. Iowa has blocked two punts, a field goal, and an extra point this season; all were returned for scores.

"Obviously, special teams were extremely big," said Iowa coach Kirk Ferentz after the win over Purdue. "That's a great weapon, when you can get the block and score off it, that's tremendous."

The contributions of the special teams are rarely as apparent as they were against the Boilermakers. Naturally, a blocked extra point returned for two points will make the evening news. But when was the last time *SportsCenter* showed highlights of really good kickoff coverage or great punt protection? Executing the unglamorous plays on special teams often leaves the opposition with bad field position, making the defense's job easier and getting the offense back on the attack.

While the average fan might not realize the importance of special teams, the Hawkeyes are well aware of how critical the "third squad" can be.

"The coaches have always expressed the importance of special teams, and I think everyone on the team has bought into that concept," said Dallas Clark, who started on special teams before moving to tight end in 2001.

"They're not going to lose games for you, but they're definitely going to win games for you."

Not only are offensive and defensive starters respectful of their overlooked brethren, they now want to be a part of the action.

"Some of the older guys are saying, 'Man, I wish I was out there on the kickoff, that looks fun,'" said backup defensive back and special teams ace Scott Boleyn. "Before, maybe some guys looked down on it, but now a lot of guys want to get on the unit."

> " THE COACHES HAVE ALWAYS EXPRESSED THE IMPORTANCE OF SPECIAL TEAMS, AND I THINK EVERYONE ON THE TEAM HAS BOUGHT INTO THAT CONCEPT. "
>
> —SENIOR TIGHT END
> DALLAS CLARK

BELOW:
Ed Hinkle outruns Northwestern's defenders on his 58-yard punt return for a touchdown on Nov. 9. Lucas Underwood/The Daily Iowan

Boleyn, a senior walk-on who has seen limited action backing up safety Bob Sanders on defense, emerged as the leader of the special teams squad, particularly on punt and kick coverage. He is regularly the first Hawkeye to get to the returner, and rarely does he miss his man. Iowa is first in the Big Ten in kickoff coverage, allowing only 14.5 yards per return. The punt-coverage team is equally as impressive, allowing just 3.9 yards per return. The conference does not rank punt coverage, but it doesn't need to—3.9 yards is a number that speaks for itself.

The most reliable special teams player, and the most high-profile, is placekicker Nate Kaeding. As automatic as they come, Kaeding is a perfect 11-11 on field goals in 2002, including 3-3 from 50 yards and over. Against Penn

State, he banged a 55-yarder off the upright and in as time expired, a play that loomed large as the game moved to overtime. Kaeding is also 27-28 on extra points.

No team is perfect, however, and Iowa still has a few questions to answer on special teams. Ferentz experimented with different punt returners during the nonconference season, ultimately settling on freshman wideout Ed Hinkel. Although Hinkel struggled early on, muffing punts against Miami of Ohio and Utah State, Ferentz doesn't foresee any more changes in the near future.

"Ed had a bump in the road early on, but he's coming along well," he said. "I'm confident that he'll be a good punt returner back there for three or four years."

The other question mark comes at the other end of the spectrum, punter David Bradley. Bradley, who had a mediocre 36.7 yards-per-punt average in 2001, has rebounded this season, raising that number to 39.7. What is cause for alarm is his performance the past two games.

Against Penn State, Bradley averaged a respectable 39, but he shanked one 13 yards on a crucial fourth-quarter attempt. The Nittany Lions took over on Iowa's 44 and scored one play later. Nothing so glaring happened against Purdue, but Bradley averaged only 34.1 that game. If that number continues to fall, Iowa could find itself on the short end of some close games.

"David hasn't been as sharp, there's no question," said Ferentz. "I'm confident he'll work through it. To me, he's a much different punter this year from what he was last year."

Finally, there's the matter of revenge. In last year's Michigan State-Iowa battle, Spartan Herb Haygood returned a kickoff 100 yards for a touchdown, the turning point in MSU's 31-28 win. The Hawkeye offensive line exorcised its 2001 demons last week by beating the Boilermakers; now special teams will have its chance to even the score.

LEFT:

Iowa junior defensive back Jermire Roberts chases a Minnesota kick returner on Nov. 16. Curtis Lehmkuhl/ The Daily Iowan

SATURDAY, OCTOBER 26, 2002

IOWA HAWKEYES 34 AT MICHIGAN WOLVERINES 9

A BLOWOUT IN THE 'BIG HOUSE'

Iowa hands the Wolverines their worst loss in Michigan Stadium since 1967, 34-9

BY TODD BROMMELKAMP
DAILY IOWAN ASSISTANT SPORTS EDITOR

ANN ARBOR, Mich.— For one day the Iowa Hawkeyes made Michigan's vaunted "Big House" their own personal fun house.

Powered by 399 yards in total offense and a relentless defense, the No. 13 Hawkeyes solidified their status as serious Big Ten title contenders with a 34-9 pasting of the No. 8 Wolverines in front of 111,496 stunned fans.

"I'm smelling the roses," said Iowa wide receiver C. J. Jones, who had a game-high 81 yards of receiving and caught two touchdown passes.

The Michigan loss, its worst at home since 1967, leaves Iowa and Ohio State as the only remaining undefeated teams in league play with just four weeks remaining in the regular season. Ohio State was defeating Penn State,13-7, in the fourth quarter at the time this story was posted.

Iowa's Bob Sanders and Jonathan Babineaux showered head coach Kirk Ferentz with Gatorade, and the Hawkeyes gathered in the south end zone of Michigan Stadium jubilantly singing the school's fight song along with several thousand Hawkeye fans shortly after time expired.

Who could blame the Hawkeyes for celebrating? The win was just Iowa's ninth in the 50-game series and its first in Ann Arbor since a 24-23 victory in 1990.

The only time this game was that close was after Michigan recovered a fumbled punt by Iowa's David Bradley on the one-yard line near the end of the first half. Michigan's Chris Perry punched the ball in two plays later, and the Wolverines added a field goal early in the third quarter to pull within one

RIGHT:

Hawkeyes running back Jermelle Lewis breaks a tackle on his way to the end zone. Zach Boyden-Holmes/The Daily Iowan

" WE JUST HAD A BIG STOP AND WERE GETTING THE BALL BACK, AND TO GIVE THEM A SHORT FIELD LIKE THAT HURT. "

—MICHIGAN LINEBACKER
VICTOR HOBSON

ABOVE:

Dallas Clark takes a pack of Michigan defenders for a ride during the Hawkeyes' win over Michigan. Zach Boyden-Holmes/The Daily Iowan

point with the score 10-9. Bradley had gotten a clean punt off earlier but offsetting penalties nullified the play.

"That's one play," Ferentz said. "Take that play away and [Bradley] played one heck of a game today.

"It's kind of like our football team—a little symbolism maybe."

Michigan managed to muster only 171 yards of total offense against the Hawkeyes, including just 62 on the ground.

In the words of Michigan coach Lloyd Carr, the Hawkeyes played a "tremendous" game.

Iowa jumped to an early 10-0 lead after quarterback Brad Banks led the Hawkeyes on an 80-yard opening drive, capped by a 39-yard screen pass to Jones for a score. Banks was a perfect five of five passing in the series and completed his first eight attempts of the day.

"I saw [the defender] wasn't looking so I thought 'All right, I'm gonna try him,'" Banks said of the play.

Nate Kaeding added a 19-yard field goal on Iowa's next possession to expand the lead, but the critical juncture in the game came in between the two scores with Michigan on offense. On just the fourth play of the game, Iowa's

BELOW:
Michigan's Marlin Jackson dives for a tackle against Iowa running back Fred Russell.
Zach Boyden-Holmes/The Daily Iowan

	1st	2nd	3rd	4th	Final
IOWA	10	0	14	10	34
MICHIGAN	0	6	3	0	9

SCORING SUMMARY

QTR	TEAM	PLAY		TIME
1st	**HAWKEYES**	TD	Jones 39-yd. pass from Banks (Kaeding kick)	10:37
1st	**HAWKEYES**	FG	Kaeding 19-yd.	3:12
2nd	**WOLVERINES**	TD	Perry 1-yd. run (missed kick)	1:13
3rd	**WOLVERINES**	FG	Finley 40-yd	12:31
3rd	**HAWKEYES**	TD	Jones 3-yd. pass from Banks (Kaeding kick)	8:57
3rd	**HAWKEYES**	TD	Lewis 5-yd. run (Kaeding kick)	2:58
4th	**HAWKEYES**	TD	Lewis 23-yd. pass from Banks (Kaeding kick)	14:47
4th	**HAWKEYES**	FG	Kaeding 27-yd.	2:49

OFFENSE

HAWKEYES

PASSING	ATT	COMP	YDS	INT	TD
Banks	29	18	222	0	3

RECEIVING	CATCHES	YDS	TD
Jones	8	81	2
Clark	5	68	0
Brown	3	41	0
Lewis	2	32	1

RUSHING	RUSHES	YDS	TD
Lewis	18	109	1
Banks	7	53	0
Russell	20	28	0
Cervantes	1	4	0
Bradley	1	-11	0

WOLVERINES

PASSING	ATT	COMP	YDS	INT	TD
Navarre	33	14	112	0	0
Brinton	6	3	37	0	0

RECEIVING	CATCHES	YDS	TD
Edwards	5	69	0
Joppru	4	45	0
Askew	3	7	0
Butler	2	12	0
Perry	2	6	0
Bellamy	1	10	0

RUSHING	RUSHES	YDS	TD
Navarre	5	18	0
Perry	9	14	1
Askew	3	-2	0
Brinton	3	-8	0

ABOVE:
Herky whips up the crowd of Iowa fans with roses, in reference to Iowa's shot at going to the Rose Bowl.
Zach Boyden-Holmes/The Daily Iowan

Colin Cole laid Michigan quarterback John Navarre on his back, momentarily knocking Navarre from the game. The junior quarterback would return two plays later, but he was never the same.

"He didn't seem like he was very comfortable back there [after that]," Cole said.

Navarre was sacked five times for a loss of 34 yards, including twice by Iowa defensive end Howard Hodges.

"The thing I was most disappointed with was we had trouble protecting the quarterback," Carr said.

Banks, meanwhile, was as comfortable as a baby in its mother's arms under center for the Hawkeyes. The senior completed 18 of 29 attempts for 222 yards, including three touchdowns, and rushed for 53 yards.

The Iowa offense seemed to sputter after its quick start but found its footing once again in the third quarter, thanks to a little help from the special teams unit. After being forced to punt on its first possession, Michigan's Markus Curry fumbled the punt after being hit by Sanders. Iowa's Scott Boleyn picked the ball up on the

" I'M SMELLING THE ROSES. "

—IOWA WIDE RECEIVER C. J. JONES

ABOVE:
*Hawkeyes receiver C. J. Jones sprints past the grasp of Wolverines'
defensive lineman Norman Heuer. Zach Boyden-Holmes/The Daily Iowan*

ABOVE:
Eric Rothwell celebrates with fans after the Hawkeyes top the Wolverines.
Zach Boyden-Holmes/The Daily Iowan

14-yard line and Iowa had new life deep in Michigan territory. It was a turning point similar to what happened when the two teams met a year ago in Iowa City, when momentum swung in Michigan's favor after a blocked punt in Iowa's end zone.

"We just had a big stop and were getting the ball back, and to give them a short field like that hurt," Michigan linebacker Victor Hobson said.

Banks made short work of the possession by hitting Jones with a three-yard pass on the third play of the drive to expand Iowa's lead to 17-9. Iowa would also score on its next two possessions after back-to-back touchdowns by Jermelle Lewis from five and 23 yards out increased Iowa's lead to 31-9.

Kaeding added a late field goal from 27 yards out to provide the final margin of victory. His perfect day extended his streak of consecutive field goal attempts to 20.

Lewis, who came on in place of an injured Fred Russell, finished the day with 109 yards rushing on 18 carries. He also had two receptions for 32 yards, including the 23-yard run, which came on an option from Banks.

"I just wanted to keep pounding it at them," Lewis said.

Russell had just 28 yards on 20 carries before leaving the game in the third quarter with a hand injury. He said he does not expect to miss any playing time.

GAME9

" I JUST WANTED TO KEEP
POUNDING IT AT THEM. "

—IOWA RUNNING BACK JERMELLE LEWIS

ABOVE:
Iowa running back Jermelle Lewis rushed for 109 yards against Michigan. Zach Boyden-Holmes/The Daily Iowan

117

Zach Boyden-Holmes/The Daily Iowan

SATURDAY, NOVEMBER 2, 2002
WISCONSIN BADGERS 3 AT IOWA HAWKEYES 20

HAWKS BUCK BUCKY, 20-3

Start Big Ten play 6-0 for first time ever

BY TODD BROMMELKAMP
DAILY IOWAN ASSISTANT SPORTS EDITOR

A special season got just a touch more special Saturday afternoon in Kinnick Stadium.

Iowa improved to 6-0 in the Big Ten for the first time in school history with a 20-3 victory over Wisconsin. The win keeps Iowa in the thick of the Big Ten championship race along with undefeated Ohio State.

The victory also snapped a five-game skid against the Badgers dating back to 1997 and gave Iowa head coach Kirk Ferentz his first victory against fellow former Iowa assistant and current Wisconsin coach Barry Alvarez.

"We were beaten by a very good football team," said Alvarez, who coached linebackers at Iowa from 1979-1986. "They have no weaknesses."

Especially when it comes to stopping the run. Iowa held Wisconsin's Anthony Davis to a career-low 16 carries for 34 yards. As a team the Badgers managed just 78 yards against the nation's second most effective run defense.

BELOW: Hawkeyes receiver Ed Hinkel takes Chuckie Cowans for a ride as he breaks free from a tackle.
Zach Boyden-Holmes/The Daily Iowan

ABOVE:
Hawkeyes Maurice Brown (left) and
Robert Gallery embrace after an Iowa
touchdown. Adam Bloom/The Daily Iowan

"Plan B is if you can't run it you try to throw," Alvarez said. "That didn't work either."

Nothing seemed to work for the Badgers against the Hawkeyes, who totaled 405 yards of offense against Wisconsin en route to the victory. Quarterback Brad Banks's stock continues to rise. He completed 17 of 30 passes for a career-high 275 yards with two touchdowns.

"I do know this, he's All-Iowa," Ferentz said when asked about Banks possibly earning national recognition at season's end. "I'm pretty sure we wouldn't trade him for anyone."

Banks has tossed 20 touchdown passes this season, just seven behind Chuck Long's school record of 27 set during the Hawkeyes' magical 1985 campaign. The senior had little trouble finding the open man against a defense that often featured eight or nine men in the box in an attempt to stop the run.

Banks hit a wide-open Maurice Brown in the end zone with just over a minute remaining in the first half to give the Hawkeyes a 10-3 halftime lead. The 21-yard pass was the only touchdown scored in a first half that saw

> " WE WERE BEATEN BY A VERY GOOD
> FOOTBALL TEAM. THEY HAVE NO WEAKNESSES. "
>
> —WISCONSIN COACH BARRY ALVAREZ

BELOW:
Iowa's Matt Roth celebrates after recording a sack on Wisconsin quarterback Brooks Bollinger.
Zach Boyden-Holmes/The Daily Iowan

	1st	2nd	3rd	4th	Final
WISCONSIN	0	3	0	0	3
IOWA	0	10	10	0	20

SCORING SUMMARY

QTR	TEAM	PLAY		TIME
2nd	**HAWKEYES**	FG	Kaeding 32-yd.	10:45
2nd	**BADGERS**	FG	Allen 26-yd.	6:21
2nd	**HAWKEYES**	TD	Brown 21-yd. pass from Banks (Kaeding kick)	1:03
3rd	**HAWKEYES**	FG	Kaeding 30-yd.	10:05
3rd	**HAWKEYES**	TD	Clark 23-yd. pass from Banks (Kaeding kick)	6:25

——— **OFFENSE** ———

BADGERS

PASSING	ATT	COMP	YDS	INT	TD
Sorgi	17	8	84	1	0
Bollinger	9	2	46	0	0
Daniels	4	1	7	1	0

RECEIVING	CATCHES	YDS	TD
Orr	6	83	0
Williams	3	45	0
Charles	1	6	0
Davis	1	3	0

RUSHING	RUSHES	YDS	TD
Davis	16	34	0
Daniels	4	18	0
Smith	4	14	0
Bollinger	6	6	0
Sorgi	3	6	0

HAWKEYES

PASSING	ATT	COMP	YDS	INT	TD
Banks	30	17	275	0	2

RECEIVING	CATCHES	YDS	TD
Brown	6	107	1
Clark	5	97	1
Jones	2	37	0
Hinkel	2	23	0
Solomon	1	6	0
Lewis	1	5	0

RUSHING	RUSHES	YDS	TD
Lewis	25	81	0
Banks	9	36	0
Cervantes	2	16	0

both teams struggle to feel each other out. Wisconsin kept Iowa off-balance for most of the half by featuring new defenses the Hawkeyes had not seen on tape. The Badgers, however, just struggled to find their footing.

A 26-yard Mike Allen field goal midway through the second quarter tied the score at 3-3 after Iowa's Nate Kaeding hit on an attempt from 32 yards out. It was the only offense Wisconsin would manage to post. The Badgers managed just 215 total yards of offense against an Iowa defense that relentlessly attacked its opponent with a vigor which caused Ferentz to hearken back to days past.

"Our guys like to hit," he said.

"That's been a Hawkeye tradition, one that we're starting to pick up again."

One of those hits was a vicious, yet clean, helmet-to-helmet hit by Derek Pagel on Wisconsin quarterback Brooks Bollinger. Bollinger, who has a history of concussions, never returned to the game and Alvarez said the senior would be examined by a doctor later in the day.

"We try to be as physical as we can," said Pagel, who also hauled in his team-leading fourth interception in the fourth quarter.

The defense also did damage to Bollinger's backup, Jim Sorgi, causing Alvarez to turn to third-stringer Owen Daniels. Sorgi, who was eight of 17 for 84 yards, reinjured his throwing hand and returned to the game but was pulled in the fourth quarter for Daniels. Alvarez said the move was made to ensure that Sorgi would be available for Wisconsin's game next week should Bollinger not be healthy.

"If you play on defense and you're not a guy who likes to hit, you're on the wrong side of the ball," said

BELOW:
Wisconsin's Own Daniels rushes to avoid Iowa defender Fabian Dodd. Adam Bloom/The Daily Iowan

RIGHT:
Iowa's Jermelle Lewis breaks through the pack against Wisconsin. Lewis gained 81 yards on 25 carries. Zach Boyden-Holmes/The Daily Iowan

tackle Colin Cole, whose hit a week ago on Michigan quarterback John Navarre set the tone for that victory.

Iowa added a 30-yard field goal by Kaeding in the third quarter to extend the lead to 13-3. Kaeding would later miss from 27 yards out, ending his school record streak of consecutive made field goals at 22. It was the only stumble Iowa experienced as it took another giant step toward a possible Big Ten championship and Rose Bowl berth.

"I hit it pretty well," Kaeding said of the attempt from the right hash mark, which sailed just over the right upright. "I put a lot of pride and pressure into every kick. I understand that I was really fortunate [with the streak]."

Banks later hit tight end Dallas Clark on a "jail-break screen" for Iowa's final score of the day. The 23-yard reception was one of five for Clark, who finished the day with 97 yards. Brown had a team-high six receptions for 107 yards.

The Badgers also had a hard time stopping Iowa's running game, as the Hawkeyes ran up 130 yards rushing. Jermelle Lewis, starting in place of the injured Fred Russell, carried 25 times for 81 yards. Banks, who was sacked three times, still managed 36 yards on nine carries. Russell, who watched from the sidelines and was not dressed, will probably return to action in time for Iowa's home finale next weekend with Northwestern, Ferentz said.

"We just felt like it was the best thing to do for all parties," Ferentz said of resting Russell.

The Hawkeyes now focus their attention on preparing for Northwestern next weekend. The Wildcats defeated Indiana for their first Big Ten victory of the season.

"[This season] has been really enjoyable," said center Bruce Nelson.

"I just hope we can ride it out these next two weeks."

BELOW:

Edgar Cervantes sets a block for Jermelle Lewis against Wisconsin.
Adam Bloom/The Daily Iowan

ABOVE:
Hawkeyes tight end Dallas Clark marches into the end zone.
Zach Boyden-Holmes/The Daily Iowan

9

BY BRIAN TRIPLETT, DAILY IOWAN REPORTER

MAURICE BROWN

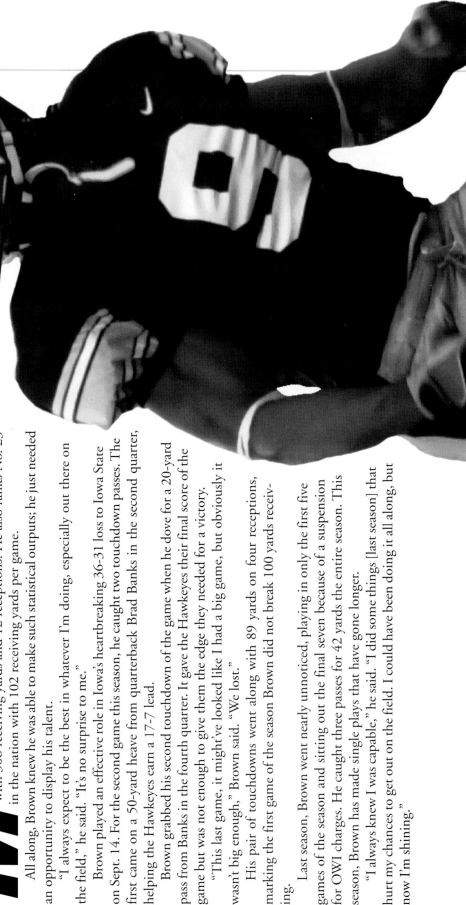

Maurice Brown emerging as the Hawkeyes' No. 1 receiver this season may be a surprise to some, but it does not come as a surprise to Maurice Brown.

The 6'2", 210-pound junior is having an exceptional year, leading the team with 306 receiving yards and 12 receptions. He also ranks No. 23 in the nation with 102 receiving yards per game.

All along, Brown knew he was able to make such statistical outputs; he just needed an opportunity to display his talent.

"I always expect to be the best in whatever I'm doing, especially out there on the field," he said. "It's no surprise to me."

Brown played an effective role in Iowa's heartbreaking 36-31 loss to Iowa State on Sept. 14. For the second game this season, he caught two touchdown passes. The first came on a 50-yard heave from quarterback Brad Banks in the second quarter, helping the Hawkeyes earn a 17-7 lead.

Brown grabbed his second touchdown of the game when he dove for a 20-yard pass from Banks in the fourth quarter. It gave the Hawkeyes their final score of the game but was not enough to give them the edge they needed for a victory.

"This last game, it might've looked like I had a big game, but obviously it wasn't big enough," Brown said. "We lost."

His pair of touchdowns went along with 89 yards on four receptions, marking the first game of the season Brown did not break 100 yards receiving.

Last season, Brown went nearly unnoticed, playing in only the first five games of the season and sitting out the final seven because of a suspension for OWI charges. He caught three passes for 42 yards the entire season. This season, Brown has made single plays that have gone longer.

"I always knew I was capable," he said. "I did some things [last season] that hurt my chances to get out on the field. I could have been doing it all along, but now I'm shining."

Zach Boyden-Holmes/The Daily Iowan

WIDE RECEIVER

HOMETOWN: FT. LAUDERDALE, FL

AGE: 21

CLASS: JR.

This year, Brown is more mature—he accepts blame for losses and values every minute on the field. Although Brown is still not listed as the Hawkeyes' No. 1 receiver—C. J. Jones still holds the official spot—he acts the part.

"I'm going to get playing time," Brown said. "When I get out there, I'm just going to make the most of it."

Brown seems to be making the most of his playing time this season. Against Akron, he scored on two first-quarter passes from Banks on 56- and 36-yard catches, ending with a career-best 102 yards.

Against Miami of Ohio, Brown tacked up 115 yards receiving to break his record from the previous week.

"[Brown] has really stepped up," said Iowa coach Kirk Ferentz.

"We had high hopes that Mo would develop into a real fine Big Ten receiver, and I think he's intent on doing that."

Brown's four touchdowns this season tie running backs Fred Russell and Jermelle Lewis's numbers for the team high.

Before the season, the three were considered an unlikely cast of characters to take control of this year's offense. But Russell and Lewis have been receiving the bulk of the playing time because of an ankle injury suffered by Aaron Greving in the preseason.

As for Brown, he made his mark in Week 1 and has been putting up numbers ever since.

"He's emerged as a guy who's gonna make the plays when they're there. He's doing a good job, so we're real happy about that," Ferentz said. "Nature will take its course, but we're real pleased with his progress."

129

FRIDAY, NOVEMBER 8, 2002

Seniors survive to finally flourish

Graduating group experiences highs and lows during time in Iowa City

BY TODD BROMMELKAMP
DAILY IOWAN ASSISTANT SPORTS EDITOR

They came from various backgrounds and will take many different paths once the season is finished, but the many seniors on the Iowa football team have at least two things in common with one another.

All 24 members of the Hawkeyes who will take the field for their final home game against Northwestern were a part of one of the greatest turnarounds in Iowa football history. And they will always be Hawkeyes.

"Hopefully, it's just going to get better when we leave," said offensive lineman Andy Lightfoot. "The young guys will step in there and be even better than we are."

That's hoping for a lot, because it would be hard to imagine a group of players that could possibly have as big an impact as the 2002 seniors did.

They arrived on campus at different times, most as redshirts in 1998, some as true freshmen in 1999, and one—offensive lineman Ben Sobieski—has lingered in Iowa City since 1997. But all stepped into the same situation, and it wasn't a good one.

Iowa went 3-8 in 1998 during the last year of head coach Hayden Fry's 20 seasons. Kirk Ferentz, who was an assistant under Fry during the 1980s, returned to Iowa City to begin the rebuilding process. It was slow and at times painful to watch.

A young, inexperienced squad took plenty of lumps during that season. Many of today's seniors, such as linebacker Fred Barr, were thrown to the wolves as true freshmen.

"We had nothing to lose," Barr said.

Except for games, of which Iowa lost all but one in 1999.

"Until you live through a season where you go 1-10 or 3-9, where you experience loss to the fullest, you can't really truly enjoy or understand the excitement of a victory," said Iowa center Bruce Nelson. "Or understand how much hard work went into it."

And in the end it was the hard work that players such as Nelson, who has started every game under Ferentz, put in that made the difference. It wasn't always apparent

Strip Photos by Curtis Lehmkuhl, Lucas Underwood, and Ben Plank

" *HOPEFULLY, IT'S JUST GOING TO GET BETTER WHEN WE LEAVE. THE YOUNG GUYS WILL STEP IN THERE AND BE EVEN BETTER THAN WE ARE.* "

—Senior Offensive Lineman
Andy Lightfoot

on the field, where the Hawkeyes were often overpowered and out-manned by the opposition, but it was there.

"That's what makes the victories now so special," Nelson said.

Iowa rebounded to go 3-9 in 2000 with Big Ten victories over Michigan State, Penn State, and Northwestern. It wasn't pretty, but it was progress.

The following season the Hawkeyes had plenty of ups and downs en route to a 7-5 finish. They finished on a definite up with a 19-16 victory over Texas Tech in the Alamo Bowl, with the 2001 seniors promising the best was yet to come.

And it was.

With just two games remaining in the regular season the Hawkeyes are poised to garner their first Big Ten championship since 1990, and a lot of the credit goes to the seniors on the team.

From transfers such as quarterback Brad Banks and wide receiver C. J. Jones, who spent just two years at Iowa, to players such as Barr and Colin Cole, who played as true freshmen, they are hungry to finish what they started what seems like ages ago.

Each one has his own unique story. Barr and Cole nearly left Iowa as true freshmen, both homesick for their native Florida.

Safeties Derek Pagel and Scott Boleyn also had thoughts of ending their walk-on careers before both decided to stick things out.

Lightfoot and fellow offensive lineman David Porter are eyeing careers in the medical world.

Porter and Sobieski, both of whom could have left Iowa after using up their eligibility, instead chose to petition for medical hardship waivers.

The National Football League will most likely call on offensive linemen Porter, Eric Steinbach, and Bruce Nelson as well as other members of the team to play on Sundays rather than Saturdays.

Still others such as Will Lack and Jason Hoveland, both walk-ons who rarely if ever saw game action, played integral parts in Iowa's success through their performances in countless practices. They paid their own way and paid their dues and are every bit as responsible for the state of the program today as any player with a scholarship.

ABOVE:
Hawkeyes senior quarterback Brad Banks slaps hands with fans after Iowa's overtime win at Penn State.
Zach Boyden-Holmes/The Daily Iowan

At one point in time, most likely during those lean years of 1999 and 2000, each and every one of the 24 players taking the field today must have asked themselves if it was all worth it. This season has provided them with a resounding answer.

But one lingering question remained. Would they trade all of their experiences, the good and the bad, for anything in the world?

"I can't imagine that," Lightfoot said.

Saturday will be an emotional day at Kinnick Stadium. Banks said he wouldn't be surprised if he "broke off a tear or two" when he walked down the steps from the Iowa locker room and the team formed "the swarm" one last time. Even Barr, perhaps the toughest man on the team, said a breakdown was inevitable.

Ferentz declined to heap accolades on the senior class, just as he has with any other group of men playing their final game for him.

"Our players have been fantastic," he said. "I'm sorry to see all of them go."

But these seniors have proved time and time again that they don't need words or anything else to justify what they have accomplished. Their progress says it all.

"I listen to a lot of people come back and speak and they have a lot to say," Barr said. "But I don't think many of them helped take a team from 1-10 and reverse that to where we could be 11-1."

RIGHT:
Hawkeye defender D. J. Johnson breaks up a pass intended for Wisconsin's Enrique Cook.
Zach Boyden-Holmes/The Daily Iowan

SATURDAY, NOVEMBER 9, 2002

NORTHWESTERN WILDCATS 10 AT IOWA HAWKEYES 62

SENIORS LEAVE KINNICK IN STYLE; WHIP WILDCATS 62-10

Iowa one win away from first Big Ten championship since 1990

BY TODD BROMMELKAMP
DAILY IOWAN ASSISTANT SPORTS EDITOR

The game was over almost before it started, but the end result was just as satisfying for the 24 seniors playing their final game in Kinnick Stadium on Saturday.

The Hawkeyes completely overwhelmed an underwhelming Northwestern team on Senior Day, cruising to a 62-10 victory. In the process, Iowa remained in the hunt for at least a share of the Big Ten title with Ohio State pending the outcome of the remaining two weeks of play.

The Buckeyes rallied to defeat Purdue, 10-3, in the final minute of their game Saturday, remaining in the driver's seat for a Rose Bowl berth.

"We're thinking about the Big Ten championship—that's the biggest thing on our minds right now," said senior defensive tackle Colin Cole. "We want that ring and then whatever bowl we go to, we'll be satisfied."

BELOW: *Iowa defenders Antwan Allen and Jovon Johnson congratulate Jonathan Babineaux after his third-quarter interception.* Lucas Underwood/The Daily Iowan

ABOVE:
*Iowa's Abdul Hodge brings down Northwestern running back Ashton Aikens on the one-foot line in the third quarter.*Lucas Underwood/The Daily Iowan

Iowa improves to 10-1 and a perfect 7-0 in Big Ten play. The 10 victories this season tie the school record, which was set in 1985 and equaled in 1987 and 1991.

"We're trying to make history here," said offensive lineman Robert Gallery. "We have one more week to take care of."

The Hawkeyes close out Big Ten play next weekend at Minnesota, where they will look to finish their first undefeated season since the conference schedule was expanded to eight games, as well as keep Floyd of Rosedale in Iowa City for a second season.

The lopsided score Saturday did nothing to take away from the emotions involved in the game. For a group of players that saw plenty of bad times during 1-10 and 3-9 seasons, this was the perfect ending.

"I can't [describe the feeling]," said Iowa wide receiver C. J. Jones. "This is the greatest place ever."

Playing for the last time in front of Iowa fans who immediately took to him as a junior college transfer last season, quarterback Brad Banks went out in style by completing all 10 of his pass attempts for 197 yards and three touchdowns. His perfect percentage sets a new Iowa standard for quarterbacks.

Banks also rushed for two scores while carrying five times for 54 yards before leaving the game to a standing ovation with eight minutes remaining in the third quarter.

"I thought that was wonderful," Banks said of the cheers as he raised his arms above his head as backup Nathan Chandler made his way onto the field.

Asked to rank Banks's performance on a scale of one to 10, wide receiver Maurice Brown said he would give Banks a 13. And with good reason, because Banks twice found Brown wide open for touchdown passes of 40 and 65 yards.

BELOW: Edgar Cervantes leaps over the line of scrimmage to pick up the one yard needed on third down. Iowa would go on to score on the drive. John Richard/The Daily Iowan

	1st	2nd	3rd	4th	Final
NORTHWESTERN	7	3	0	0	10
IOWA	14	21	21	6	62

SCORING SUMMARY

QTR	TEAM	PLAY		TIME
1st	**HAWKEYES**	TD	Lewis 7-yd. run (Kaeding kick)	12:22
1st	**HAWKEYES**	TD	Brown 40-yd. pass from Banks (Kaeding kick)	10:45
1st	**WILDCATS**	TD	Aikens 8-yd. pass from Basanez (Wasielewski kick)	8:18
2nd	**HAWKEYES**	TD	Banks 9-yd. run (Kaeding kick)	12:28
2nd	**HAWKEYES**	TD	Brown 65-yd. pass from Banks (Kaeding kick)	10:19
2nd	**WILDCATS**	FG	Wasielewski 26-yd.	5:21
2nd	**HAWKEYES**	TD	Banks 19-yd. run (Kaeding kick)	2:18
3rd	**HAWKEYES**	TD	Hinkel punt return (Kaeding kick)	13:18
3rd	**HAWKEYES**	TD	Clark 28-yd. pass from Banks (Kaeding kick)	9:36
3rd	**HAWKEYES**	TD	Jones 22-yd. pass from Chandler (Kaeding kick)	6:43
4th	**HAWKEYES**	TD	Schnoor 5-yd. run (Molinaro kick failed)	12:49

OFFENSE

WILDCATS

PASSING	ATT	COMP	YDS	INT	TD
Basanez	29	19	166	1	1
Stauss	8	5	33	0	0
Jenkins	4	0	0	2	0

RECEIVING	CATCHES	YDS	TD
Patrick	5	63	0
Philmore	3	29	0
Wright	4	27	0
Backes	2	19	0
Schweighardt	3	19	0
Jordan	2	15	0
Aikens	2	13	1
Lawrence	2	10	0
Foster	1	4	0

RUSHING	RUSHES	YDS	TD
Lawrence	6	37	0
Wright	11	32	0
Jenkins	7	19	0
Herron	5	13	0
Stauss	1	4	0
Basanez	6	-3	0

HAWKEYES

PASSING	ATT	COMP	YDS	INT	TD
Banks	10	10	197	0	3
Chandler	2	2	33	0	1

RECEIVING	CATCHES	YDS	TD
Brown	4	129	2
Clark	3	45	1
Jones	3	37	1
Mickens	1	11	0
Jensen	1	8	0

RUSHING	RUSHES	YDS	TD
Russell	17	100	0
Banks	5	54	2
Lewis	12	50	1
Schnoor	8	32	1
Cervantes	2	12	0
Sherlock	2	4	0
Chandler	1	1	0
Mickens	3	-8	0

"I don't know if they even knew Mo was out there," said Banks, whose trio of touchdown passes leaves him just four shy of Chuck Long's season record of 27, set in 1985.

But Banks, like most everybody else inside Kinnick Stadium, credited the performance of Iowa's offensive line for the victory. All five seniors on the line—David Porter, Ben Sobieski, Eric Steinbach, Bruce Nelson, and Andy Lightfoot—walked off the field to a deafening roar during the third quarter, spontaneously holding hands as their second-string counterparts raced to the huddle.

"We didn't plan on holding hands or anything," said Sobieski, a sixth-year senior who has been a part of three Senior Days. "It was a great moment."

Even Ferentz, who normally shies away from such things as curtain calls, got emotional when speaking about the line's exit from the game.

"Senior day is tough on me," he said as his eyes reddened. "Believe it or not, I'm an emotional guy and senior day has always been hard on me."

But saying goodbye to an offensive line which has served as the bread and butter of this team was extra tough on Ferentz, a former offensive line coach.

"It kind of typifies the way our careers have gone," said center Bruce Nelson. "We've grown up together and we've played together, and we've learned a lot about football and life at the same time."

BELOW:
Iowa freshman wide receiver Ed Hinkel celebrates after he returned a punt for a touchdown.
Lucas Underwood/The Daily Iowan

RIGHT:
Iowa fans voice their opinions as to who is the best of the Big Ten's undefeated teams.
John Richard/The Daily Iowan

All 24 of Iowa's seniors, with the exception of quarterback David Raih, who is recovering from shoulder surgery, saw playing time at some point during the rout, which began with a seven-yard touchdown run by Jermelle Lewis and ended with a five-yard run by running back Marcus Schnoor.

"They took it to us in every aspect of the game," said Northwestern coach Randy Walker. "We took some chances coming out of the blocks; we felt they were a good enough team we had to do that."

Lewis's touchdown run occurred on Iowa's opening drive, which was set up when the Wildcats opened the game with an onside kick attempt which failed miserably. On Northwestern's ensuing possession, a mix-up between Walker and his staff caused the Wildcats to run a play on fourth and one, which resulted in turning the ball over to Iowa on its own 42. Two plays later, Banks found Brown from 40 yards out, and the rout was on.

"This has been the funnest season," said Brown, who along with Jones is now just one touchdown shy of Quinn Early's single-season record of 10 set in 1987. Brown finished the day with 129 yards on four receptions, marking the fifth time this season he has eclipsed the 100-yard mark. Jones had 37 yards on three catches.

Running back Fred Russell also eclipsed the 100-yard mark in rushing with exactly 100 yards on 17 attempts. His daily total moved him past the 1,000-yard mark this season to 1,025, making him the 10th Hawkeye to rush for over 1,000 yards.

"It was tough to get to 1,000," said Russell, who has battled injuries this season. "But it was a nice feeling."

Defensively, Iowa held the Wildcats to just 298 yards and one touchdown, an eight-yard pass from Brett Basanez to Ashton Aikens, which made the game 14-7 in the first quarter. The Wildcats also added a 26-yard field goal by David Wasielewski in the second quarter.

Safety Scott Boleyn, a walk-on playing in his final game in Iowa City, recorded two interceptions. Defensive end Jonathan Babineaux also had an interception after linebacker Abdul Hodge tipped a Basanez pass at the line of scrimmage.

With Iowa leading 35-10 at halftime, Ed Hinkel returned a punt 58 yards for a touchdown following Northwestern's first possession of the half. During Iowa's next possession, Banks found tight end Dallas Clark for a 28-yard scoring strike to move the game even further out of reach.

The Hawkeyes now turn their attention to Minnesota, Iowa's final Big Ten opponent this season. Regardless of what Ohio State does in its final two games, a victory next weekend would assure the Hawkeyes of at least a share of their first Big Ten championship since 1990.

"We just want to make sure we get our next game out of the way," Russell said. "We know how important these games are; we just need to stay focused."

Added an emotional Cole,""Nobody on this team can say they've won a Big Ten title."

WE'RE THINKING ABOUT THE BIG TEN CHAMPIONSHIP—THAT'S THE BIGGEST THING ON OUR MINDS RIGHT NOW. WE WANT THAT RING AND THEN WHATEVER BOWL WE GO TO, WE'LL BE SATISFIED.

BELOW:

Hawkeyes running back Fred Russell looks for room to maneuver against Northwestern. Russell gained 100 yards on 17 carries to surpass 1,000 for the season. Lucas Underwood/The Daily Iowan

BRAD BANKS

7

BY DONOVAN BURBA, DAILY IOWAN SPORTS WRITER

The press room at legendary Kinnick Stadium was nearly empty by the time the sun started to set on Nov. 9. Outside, postgame tailgate parties were in full swing, but calm reigned in the bowels of the venerable brick structure. A half-hour earlier, Brad Banks stood surrounded by a dozen television cameras and twice that many reporters, but now only a handful remained. Just as Banks wrapped up his final interview, a reporter asked him to "strike the pose."

Banks, normally reserved and quiet off the field, doubled over with laughter, then gave his best Heisman impression. He may have found the request funny, but his candidacy for sports' most prestigious award is no joke.

To say that Banks wasn't considered a Heisman candidate at the start of the season is an understatement; only recently has he been acknowledged as the best quarterback in Iowa. Although he was solid backing up Kyle McCann last year, Banks still entered 2002 with a question mark on his back. Would he play up to fans' expectations, turning into a multifaceted threat like Iowa State's Seneca Wallace? Or would his perceived lack of experience and patience make the team's most important position its most obvious weakness?

It took Banks, oh, 15 minutes to answer any doubters. He went 21-29 for 125 and two touchdowns (both more than 35 yards), and was off and running. Going into Iowa's final game of the season, he leads the nation in quarterback efficiency, which takes into account such factors as completion per-

Zach Boyden-Holmes/The Daily Iowan

AGE: 20

YEAR: SR.

HOMETOWN: BELLE GLADE, FL

QUARTERBACK

centage, touchdowns, and interceptions. Banks is also second in the country in yards per attempt, averaging 9.4 yards per throw. Most recently, he went 10-10 passing for 197 yards and three touchdowns and rushed for two more scores.

But only within the past few weeks has the senior garnered any national attention. Why? For starters, the national Heisman campaigns that start in the summer aren't part of the Hawkeye game plan. Iowa's alumni aren't so foolish as to pay $250,000 for billboard space in Times Square on which to advertise, as Oregon's have the past two years. That high-profile tactic made immediate Heisman contenders out of Ducks Joey Harrington and Onterrio Smith. Every time I move my computer's mouse, I caress a photo of Indiana's Antwaan Randle El, who, as the mouse pad informs me, is "A front-runner for the 2001 Heisman Trophy." At press time, Banks's face has not been emblazoned on any office supplies.

Nowhere is the air of humility more pervasive than in Iowa City. Banks is so devoted to the team's "one week at a time" mantra that following the Nov. 9 game against Northwestern, he expressed surprise, almost shock, at hearing that the Hawkeyes needed just one more win to clinch the Big Ten title. Even his Heisman pose was decidedly untrophy-like.

The Heisman hype hasn't found its way into Iowa's locker room or huddle, either.

"It's not going to affect our play calling, and it's not going to affect the way Brad prepares," said coach Kirk Ferentz. "We're just playing to give ourselves the best chance to win, not Brad the best chance to win the Heisman."

Numbers can only say so much about a player, and Banks's defining moment may have come at the season's lowest point. In the Hawkeyes' lone loss, on Sept. 14 to Iowa State, Banks fumbled the ball away on consecutive possessions, enabling the Cyclones to erase a 17-point deficit to win, 36-31. Banks easily could have broken under the criticism that came his way following the loss. Instead, he led Iowa to the top five in the polls, where the Hawkeyes haven't been in more than a decade.

Banks is certainly still an outside shot to win the Heisman, but the stars could align to give him the award. Willis McGahee and Ken Dorsey, both of Miami, are considered front-runners for the award, but neither means as much to the Hurricanes, who have one of the most talented teams ever, as Banks does to the Hawkeyes. Marshall's Byron Leftwich, the favorite for much of the season, won't play Saturday because of a shin injury. If Dorsey and McGahee split the ballot, and Leftwich drops off because of his health, Banks could be left holding the trophy Dec. 14.

"There are other good candidates out there," said Ferentz. "But to say he's not a good candidate would be silly."

RIGHT:
Iowa head coach Kirk Ferentz gets carried off the field holding a rose following the Hawkeyes' win over Minnesota. Curtis Lehmkuhl/The Daily Iowan

TUESDAY, NOVEMBER 12, 2002

Ferentz, respect: Better late than never

BY TODD BROMMELKAMP
DAILY IOWAN ASSISTANT SPORTS EDITOR

Kirk Ferentz.

What images and phrases does that name bring to mind?

Now, the better question: What did people associate with that name two or three years ago? I can guarantee you they aren't the same things, and I can assert some of them couldn't be printed here.

Things are indeed, as Ferentz said last week, much warmer and fuzzier than when Iowa suffered through a 1-10 season in 1999 and most of the way through the 3-9 campaign of 2000.

Speaking of campaigns, it brings to mind the old political maxim that if everyone who told a losing candidate they voted for them had actually done so, they would have won the election. If Adlai Stevenson were still alive, he'd explain the whole thing in painstaking detail. Needless to say, if everyone who says they supported Ferentz from day one actually had, the Internet message board business would have gone the way of the Pet Rock long ago.

The remarkable thing about Ferentz is that he is the same man today as he was when he arrived at Iowa from the Baltimore Ravens—except now, instead of having his name tossed around next to Ray Nagel and Frank Lauterbur, he's garnering mention alongside the likes of Hayden Fry and Forest Evashevski. And he is not-so-quietly drawing consideration for national Coach of the Year honors.

There is not a single coach in the nation who has done a better job of getting the most from his players on a consistent basis this season, and it would be a travesty if his accomplishments went ignored outside of Iowa. Not that Ferentz would mind being slighted—he's about as mellow off the field as the crowd at a Cheech'n' Chong marathon. But a lot of other people would be up in arms, and rightfully so.

The choice will ultimately come down to the 72 voting members of the AP who make the selection, and anytime you put something in the hands of sportswriters, it's like playing Russian roulette with only one empty chamber.

There still remains a lot of football to be played, but most agree Notre Dame coach Tyrone Willingham appears to have the inside track for numerous reasons. Some feel that if Bob Davie were still in South Bend, the Irish would have a hard time beating a high school JV team. Others are likely considering Willingham, who is now one of only three black coaches at the college game's highest level, because he would be the feel-good story of the year in the wake of Michigan State's decision to fire Bobby Williams. And some undoubtedly hold the belief that "Touchdown Jesus" would rain fire and brimstone upon the Earth if they didn't cast a vote for Notre Dame's coach whether his record was perfect, winless, or anywhere in between. And there are certainly those who are clueless enough to accidentally cast ballots for Pat Buchanan.

Another Notre Dame loss and an Iowa victory this weekend would change things dramatically, but for now,

it seems life may once again be dealing Ferentz a pair of twos from the bottom of the deck. But if there's one thing people have learned about Ferentz, it's that he has the uncanny Kenny Rogers-like ability to turn a questionable hand into a royal flush. And he's done so without anyone passing him cards under the table, pulling an ace from his sleeve, or a lucrative television contract with NBC.

Perhaps the best thing about this season, whether Ferentz wins national recognition for his efforts or not, is that he is finally being appreciated at his own school. It's unlikely Ferentz is reveling in his former detractors being forced to eat crow, but I'm sure he has a few recipes he'd enjoy sharing.

While the Hawkeyes may not see a season exactly as magical as their current one any time soon, one thing remains to be said: Things will remain warm and fuzzy for as long as Ferentz is at Iowa.

BELOW: *Iowa coach Kirk Ferentz argues with a referee late in the Indiana game over a call that extended a Hoosier drive.*
Lucas Underwood/The Daily Iowan

"*THERE IS NOT A SINGLE COACH IN THE NATION WHO HAS DONE A BETTER JOB OF GETTING THE MOST FROM HIS PLAYERS ON A CONSISTENT BASIS, AND IT WOULD BE A TRAVESTY IF HIS ACCOMPLISHMENTS WENT IGNORED OUTSIDE OF IOWA.*"

BELOW:

Iowa defensive coordinator Norm Parker, right, and head coach Kirk Ferentz look on during Iowa's 45-21 victory over Minnesota. Curtis Lehmkuhl/The Daily Iowan

ABOVE:
Iowa head coach Kirk Ferentz goes over his play list during the Hawkeyes' victory over Wisconsin. Zach Boyden-Holmes/The Daily Iowan

SATURDAY, NOVEMBER 16, 2002

IOWA HAWKEYES 45 AT MINNESOTA GOLDEN GOPHERS 21

CHAMPIONS!

Hawks destroy Gophers, 45-21; clinch title

BY TODD BROMMELKAMP
DAILY IOWAN ASSISTANT SPORTS EDITOR

MINNEAPOLIS— The Iowa Hawkeyes have finally "broken the rock."

It had been chipped, cracked, and weakened over the course of Iowa's 11-1 season this year, but Saturday at the Hubert H. Humphrey Metrodome it was completely pulverized over the course of the Hawkeyes' 45-21 victory over Minnesota.

"It's a great day for the state of Iowa," said Iowa coach Kirk Ferentz, who was carried off the field on the shoulders of his players, a rose grasped in his right hand. "I can't put this feeling into words."

An emotional Ferentz doled out praise to just about everyone he could think of, from Iowa athletics director Bob Bowlsby down to the team's video staff, following the win. Everyone, that is, except for himself.

"Everyone in Iowa should know that he is the man," said Iowa offensive lineman David Porter. "He is the reason we are where we're at today."

Where Iowa is at currently is atop the Big Ten conference at season's end for the first time since 1990. Iowa's victory over the Gophers assured the team of at

BELOW: Iowa's Clinton Solomon is congratulated by teammates following a late touchdown against Minnesota.
Curtis Lehmkuhl/The Daily Iowan

ABOVE: *Iowa linebacker Matt Roth brings down Minnesota running back Thomas Tapeh.*
Ben Plank/The Daily Iowan

least a share of the conference title and established new marks for victories in a season and in Big Ten play, something which the Hawkeyes had not done since 1922, when they played only five league games.

"Hard work pays off," said center Bruce Nelson, who credited recent former Hawkeyes as well as his current teammates for helping to lay the groundwork for Iowa's success.

As they have done all season long, Nelson and his teammates on the offensive line turned in another dominating performance, helping to pave the way for Iowa's offense to run up 465 total yards against the Gophers.

"I feel like the O-line's job is to open up holes for the running back, so you give back to them by picking up yards," said running back Jermelle Lewis.

Lewis and starter Fred Russell did a lot of giving back, combining for 295 of Iowa's 365 ground yards. Russell carried 17 times for 194 yards and one touchdown before leaving the game in the second half with an injured shoulder. Lewis rushed for 101 yards on 19 attempts and one score.

Quarterback Brad Banks did little to detract from the national attention he has garnered for himself. Banks completed nine of 17 passes for 100 yards and two touchdowns and rushed for 39 yards and two scores.

"It was a well-balanced game," Banks said. "I give credit to our blocking up front."

Banks and the Hawkeyes set the tone for an impressive day on their first possession of the game, driving 80 yards in just 2:16 and picking up four consecutive first downs before Russell reached the end zone on just the fifth play of the drive.

The quick start electrified a sellout crowd of 65,184—the largest ever for a Gopher football game at the Metrodome—an estimated 30,000 of whom were cheering on Iowa.

"Walking out here, it was like Kinnick Stadium with a roof on it," said tight end Dallas Clark of the thousands of Iowa fans who made the trip to Minneapolis.

The hostile "home" crowd helped to put the Gophers on the defensive, a position they would remain in the entire day.

ABOVE: Iowa fans celebrate at the Metrodome by tearing down the goalposts after the Hawkeyes beat the Minnesota Golden Gophers to finish the Big Ten season undefeated. Ben Plank/The Daily Iowan

It was the same with Minnesota's offense, which lost six turnovers to the Hawkeyes. Quarterback Asad Abdul-Khaliq threw two interceptions, but Minnesota's undoing came on four fumbles, three of which led to Iowa scores.

Defensive end Howard Hodges forced a pair of fumbles, including one which eventually led to a six-yard touchdown pass to Clinton Solomon, which extended Iowa's lead to 35-14 early in the third quarter. Hodges also had a sack, which caused a fumble that he recovered in the second quarter, leading to an 11-yard scamper by Banks.

Jared Clauss recovered an Abdul-Khaliq fumble on the one-yard line after Colin Cole jarred the ball loose. That led to a one-yard run by Banks for the game's final score halfway through the fourth quarter.

"We gave them a miniature field, which really put our defense in some tough situations," Mason said.

But Iowa was capable of playing with an entire field as well. Banks led Iowa on a nine-play, 72-yard drive in the second quarter, which he topped off by hitting a wide-open Mo Brown for a 31-yard scoring strike.

"He's got to be a Heisman Trophy candidate," Ferentz said of Banks.

Brown led all Iowa receivers with 41 yards on just two catches including his touchdown grab, which was his 10th this season, tying him with former NFL wide receiver Quinn Early for the most touchdown receptions in a season.

Kicker Nate Kaeding also continued his assault on the Iowa record books. Kaeding, who earlier this season set a new school record for consecutive made field goals and point-after attempts, established a new single-season record for PATs made and attempted with 55 and 56 respectively. Kaeding also set a new Iowa single-season scoring record with his 115th point of the year.

The Hawkeyes now find themselves in the rather precarious position of being able to sit back and watch the final week of Big Ten play from their couches. Since Iowa is the final conference team to enjoy a bye week, the Hawkeyes must wait until next weekend's games are over before they know exactly where they will be headed come New Year's Day.

Ohio State defeated Illinois, 23-16, in overtime Nov. 16 to remain undefeated in Big Ten play along with Iowa, but the Buckeyes must play Michigan next week in Columbus.

	1st	2nd	3rd	4th	Final
IOWA	14	14	7	10	45
MINNESOTA	7	7	7	0	21

SCORING SUMMARY

QTR	TEAM	PLAY		TIME
1st	**HAWKEYES**	TD	Russell 10-yd. run (Kaeding kick)	12:44
1st	**GOLDEN GOPHERS**	TD	Burns 11-yd. pass from Abdul-Khaliq (Nystrom kick)	1:46
1st	**HAWKEYES**	TD	Lewis 6-yd. run (Kaeding kick)	0:29
2nd	**HAWKEYES**	TD	Banks 11-yd. run (Kaeding kick)	13:22
2nd	**HAWKEYES**	TD	Brown 31-yd. pass from Banks (Kaeding kick)	7:48
2nd	**GOLDEN GOPHERS**	TD	Abdul-Khaliq 1-yd. run (Nystrom kick)	0:32
3rd	**HAWKEYES**	TD	Soloman 6-yd. pass from Banks (Kaeding kick)	11:12
3rd	**GOLDEN GOPHERS**	TD	Abdul-Khaliq 1-yd. run (Nystrom kick)	5:55
4th	**HAWKEYES**	FG	Kaeding 21-yd.	14:57
4th	**HAWKEYES**	TD	Banks 1-yd. run (Kaeding kick)	13:22

—— OFFENSE ——

HAWKEYES

PASSING	ATT	COMP	YDS	INT	TD
Banks	17	9	100	0	2

RECEIVING	CATCHES	YDS	TD
Clark	3	33	0
Brown	2	41	1
Hinkel	1	15	0
Solomon	1	6	1
Ochoa	1	5	0
Jones	1	0	0

RUSHING	RUSHES	YDS	TD
Russell	17	194	1
Lewis	19	101	1
Banks	7	39	2
Schnoor	5	27	0
Cervantes	5	16	0
Chandler	1	-4	0
Brown	2	-8	0

GOLDEN GOPHERS

PASSING	ATT	COMP	YDS	INT	TD
Abdul-Khaliq	30	18	205	2	1

RECEIVING	CATCHES	YDS	TD
Patterson	5	44	0
Burns	5	43	1
Ellerson	4	39	0
Hosack	2	61	0
Utecht	2	18	0

RUSHING	RUSHES	YDS	TD
Tapeh	16	48	0
Jackson II	5	25	0
Upchurch	2	10	0
Johnson	1	-1	0
Abdul-Khaliq	8	-2	2

ABOVE:

Iowa's Antwan Allen intercepts a pass during Iowa's 45-21 victory over Minnesota. Ben Plank/The Daily Iowan

LEFT:

Fred Russell gets caught up by a Minnesota defender. Ben Plank/The Daily Iowan

ABOVE:
Iowa quarterback Brad Banks gets caught up by a Minnestota defender. Curtis Lehmkuhl/The Daily Iowan

RIGHT:
Minnesota running back Thomas Tapeh tries to slip past Iowa defenders Antwan Allen, left, and Grant Steen. Curtis Lehmkuhl/The Daily Iowan

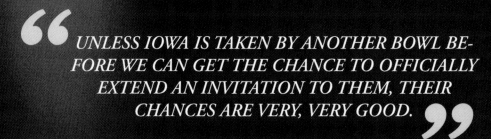

" UNLESS IOWA IS TAKEN BY ANOTHER BOWL BEFORE WE CAN GET THE CHANCE TO OFFICIALLY EXTEND AN INVITATION TO THEM, THEIR CHANCES ARE VERY, VERY GOOD. "

—FORMER ROSE BOWL PRESIDENT KEN BURROWS

RIGHT:
An Iowa fan holds a rose during the Hawkeyes game against the Golden Gophers of Minnesota.
Ben Plank/The Daily Iowan

HAWKEYES REGULAR-SEASON STATISTICS

OFFENSE

PASSING

PLAYER	ATT	CMP	PCT	YDS	TD	INT
Banks	258	155	60.1	2369	25	4
Chandler	20	12	60.0	161	1	0

RECEIVING

PLAYER	ATT	YDS	AVG	TD
Brown	42	903	21.5	10
Clark	39	645	16.5	4
Jones	36	455	12.6	9
Hinkel	19	187	9.8	1
Solomon	14	159	11.4	1
Ochoa	5	64	12.8	0
Lewis	4	48	12.0	1
Jensen	2	33	16.5	0
Jackson	2	10	5.0	0
Mickens	1	11	11.0	0
Russell	1	11	11.0	0
Cervantes	1	5	5.0	0
Greving	1	-1	-1.0	0

RUSHING

PLAYER	ATT	YDS	AVG	TD
Russell	211	1219	5.8	9
Lewis	121	678	5.6	8
Banks	73	387	5.3	5
Schnoor	29	127	4.4	1
Cervantes	25	127	5.1	1
Greving	39	120	3.1	0
Jones	2	30	15	0
Chandler	5	8	1.6	0
Mangan	1	8	8.0	0
Sherlock	4	8	2.0	0
Mickens	7	-4	-0.6	0
Brown	2	-8	-4.0	0
Bradley	1	-11	-11.0	0

SPECIAL TEAMS

FIELD GOALS

PLAYER	1-19	20-29	30-39	40-49	50+
Kaeding	1-1	6-7	5-5	5-6	3-3

PUNTING

PLAYER	NO	AVG	INSIDE 20
Bradley	48	39.2	18

PUNT RETURNS

PLAYER	NO	YDS	AVG	TD	LONG
Hinkel	27	325	12.0	1	58
Jones	3	26	8.7	0	18
Solomon	3	26	8.7	0	13
Considine	2	36	18.0	0	0
Follett	0	0	0.0	1	0
Roberts	0	0	0.0	1	0

KICKOFF RETURNS

PLAYER	NO	YDS	AVG	TD	LONG
Jones	15	337	22.5	0	50
Lewis	12	320	26.7	1	94
Cervantes	2	25	12.5	0	16
Considine	1	23	23.0	0	23

DEFENSE

TACKLES

PLAYER	NO	SOLO	AST
Barr	109	54	55
Sanders	89	59	30
Pagel	80	57	23
Cole	78	51	27
Worthy	77	34	43
Hodges	60	41	19
Allen	57	42	15
Clauss	54	28	26
Steen	53	29	24
Babineaux	52	30	22
Roth	43	19	24

PLAYER	NO	SOLO	AST
Boleyn	39	31	8
Hodge	32	24	8
D.J. Johnson	31	23	8
J. Johnson	31	23	8
Considine	23	15	8
Greenway	15	8	7
Burrier	14	6	8
Ejiasi	13	9	4
Roberts	12	6	6
Hinkel	6	1	5
Robinson	6	2	4
Follett	6	2	4
Lewis	5	4	1
Smith	5	4	1

PLAYER	NO	SOLO	AST
Dodd	4	2	2
Kaeding	4	3	1
Cervantes	3	3	0
Shelton	3	3	0
Holloway	3	2	1
Clark	3	2	1
Mickelson	2	0	2
Revak	2	1	1
Luebke	1	1	0
Neubauer	1	1	0
Gray	1	1	0
Webb	1	1	0
Helms	1	1	0
Ochoa	1	0	1
Mickens	1	1	0

SACKS

PLAYER	NO	PLAYER	NO
Hodges	9	Barr	1
Roth	9	Sanders	1
Cole	8	Allen	1
Babineaux	6	Steen	1
Clauss	5	Hodge	1
Worthy	2	Burrier	1
		Robinson	1

INTERCEPTIONS

PLAYER	NO	YDS	AVG	TD
J. Johnson	4	71	17.8	0
Pagel	4	89	22.2	1
Steen	3	17	5.7	0
Allen	2	0	0.0	0
Sanders	2	15	7.5	0
Boleyn	2	4	2.0	0
D.J. Johnson	1	19	19.0	0
Shelton	1	4	4.0	0
Babineaux	1	10	10.0	0

TEAM

	HAWKEYES	OPP
Total 1st downs	252	252
Rushing yards/game	2530	3251
Passing yards/game	210.8	270.9
3rd down: made/att.	73/160	55/176
Net Yards Rushing	2665	818
Net Yards Passing	2530	3251
Sacks	36	11
Total touchdowns	58	27
Rushing	24	13
Passing touchdowns	26	14

John Richard/The Daily Iowan

The Daily Iowan

The entire staff of the *Daily Iowan* sports and photo departments contributed to the coverage of the Hawkeyes' 2002 season. We gratefully acknowledge the efforts of:

Curtis Lehmkuhl

Ben Plank

Whitney Kidder

Lucas Underwood

John Richard

Stephanie McNiel

Donovan Burba

Brian Triplett

Danny Wilcox-Frazier

Jennifer Wagner

Celebrate the Heroes of Iowa Sports
in These Other Acclaimed Titles from Sports Publishing!

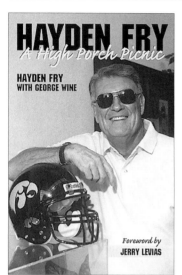

Hayden Fry: A High Porch Picnic

by Hayden Fry
with George Wine
- 6" x 9" hardcover and softcover
- 272 pages
- 32-page photo section
- $22.95 (hardcover)
- $14.95 (softcover)

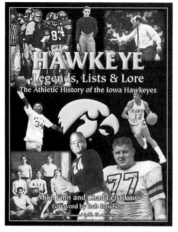

Hawkeye Legends, Lists & Lore

by Mike Finn
and Chad Leistikow
- 8.5" x 11" hardcover
- 287 pages
- eight-page color-photo section
- $34.95

2002-03 University of Iowa Basketball Guide

by the University of Iowa Sports Information Dept.
- 8.5" x 11" softcover
- 300+ pages
- photos throughout
- $20.00

Hawkeye Legends, Lists & Lore
(autographed leatherbound edition)

by Mike Finn
and Chad Leistikow
- 8.5" x 11" leatherbound
- 287 pages
- 8-pg. color-photo section
- Now $79.95! (was $129.95)
- All copies autographed by Chuck Long, Hayden Fry, Dan Gable, Jim Heffernan, Jolette Law, Angie Lee, Tom Davis, and the authors! (Certificate of Authenticity included)
- Less than 250 remain!

2002 University of Iowa Football Guide

by the University of Iowa Sports Information Dept.
- 8.5" x 11" softcover
- 300+ pages
- photos throughout
- $20.00

The Big Ten: A Century of Excellence

by Dale Ratermann
- 8.5" x 11" hardcover
- 456 pages
- eight-page color-photo section
- $39.95

To order at any time, please call toll-free **877-424-BOOK (2665)**.
For fast service and quick delivery, order on-line at
www.SportsPublishingLLC.com.